STASH-BUSTER
QUILTS

Lynne Edwards

Time-saving designs for
fabric leftovers

D&C
David and Charles

To the memory of my dear old dad, God bless him, who was the one who suggested that *Making Scrap Quilts to Use It Up* needed a sequel.

Also to the memory of Pam Kearney, a much-missed Thursday Girl, and to Hazel Hurst and Phyll Howes-Bassett, dear friends who supported and encouraged me in everything I did. These two were my fairy godmothers and I miss them hugely.

To all my family, especially my brother and his wife, who were towers of strength when I needed them.

And finally, of course, to the quilters in Chelsworth, with whom there is never a dull moment. Still no respect but I can dream …

A DAVID & CHARLES BOOK
Copyright © David & Charles Limited 2006

David & Charles is an F+W Publications Inc. company
4700 East Galbraith Road
Cincinnati, OH 45236

First published in the UK in 2006

Text and illustrations copyright © Lynne Edwards 2006

Lynne Edwards has asserted her right to be identified as author of this work in accordance with the Copyright, Designs and Patents Act, 1988.

A catalogue record for this book is available from the British Library.

ISBN-13: 978-0-7153-2194-2 hardback
ISBN-10: 0-7153-2194-3 hardback

ISBN-13: 978-0-7153-2463-9 paperback (USA only)
ISBN-10: 0-7153-2463-2 paperback (USA only)

Printed in Singapore by KHL Printing Co Pte Ltd
for David & Charles
Brunel House   Newton Abbot   Devon

Executive Editor Cheryl Brown
Editor Ame Verso
Assistant Editor Louise Clark
Head of Design Prudence Rogers
Project Editor Lin Clements
Production Controller Ros Napper

Visit our website at www.davidandcharles.co.uk

David & Charles books are available from all good bookshops; alternatively you can contact our Orderline on 0870 9908222 or write to us at FREEPOST EX2 110, D&C Direct, Newton Abbot, TQ12 4ZZ (no stamp required UK only); US customers call 800-289-0963 and Canadian customers call 800-840-5220.

Contents

The Art of Stash-Busting

For more than four years I have been focused on finding, creating and developing quilt designs that will make some inroads into the piles of fabric that have accumulated relentlessly over the years – fabric on shelves, in drawers, in boxes and in piles on the floor. But I don't need to tell you about all that. If you have been a quilter for more than a year you know exactly what I am describing. To the uninitiated eye this represents the mindless accumulation of useless stuff (we won't even touch on the capital outlay involved). But what they need to understand is that when we buy fabric we are building

and maintaining a collection. Collecting is just as much a creative activity as painting, writing novels or making quilts.

Everyone's collection is different. I don't feel a compulsion to buy autumn shades or really bright fabric. Soft shades and subtle tones of blues/greys/mauves/pinks are my areas of addiction. Our fabric choices are personal and probably colour co-ordinated and it is that element of a collection that appeals. Nevertheless, what we have to realize is that the longer a piece of fabric stays in a stash, the more it loses its power and attraction. It needs to be taken out, shaken, grouped with others that give it new life, as it gives new life to them. In other words we *have* to use some of our collection or it cannot grow and continue to give pleasure.

Don't be afraid to use the stuff: it justifies your collecting habit and after all, that's what it was made for. Reviewing my fabrics both for this book and my previous one, *Making Scrap Quilts to Use It Up,* proved to be an unexpected pleasure, like going to a family wedding or college reunion and meeting up again with people you had almost forgotten. Not only had I renewed my relationship with some lovely pieces of fabric but in using them in a quilt I have introduced them to other people who now also get a chance to enjoy seeing them.

The more I worked on quilt designs with a view to using lots of fabrics in

whatever amounts I happened to have, the more ideas seemed to appear. My students, too, were hungry for more and by the time *Making Scrap Quilts to Use It Up* had been published there were enough additional quilt designs already underway for this book. This time I have focused on techniques that are high on efficiency and time-saving features to move the design along. Not exactly 'quilt in a day' but certainly aiming at keeping the ideas bubbling and the quilt growing speedily so that the fabric stashes don't get too dusty.

I have to confess that after a long spell of controlled abstinence I have weakened several times in the past three months and bought new fabric, the designs and colours of which I couldn't resist. I've no plans to use them yet, but they are arranged artfully in a shallow basket in my workroom and I see them every day as I move about the room. All quilters will understand the pleasure that gives me. So, do not stop buying fabric – it is a part of the collecting process. Don't put your new acquisitions away or hide them from a disapproving family. You bought them to enjoy, so do just that, even if that means just stroking them occasionally. After a while, move them along and mix them with your established collections. Start cooking a new quilt project by auditioning new groupings of fabrics from your stash. A static collection grows stale: it needs to be constantly reassessed, used and replenished.

In this latest book you will find 20 projects, both large and small, to use with all that fabric. Some of the quilts have been made by me, others by my students, and the range of fabrics varied to suit the taste of each maker. We all have a little less in our stashes now – but not for long, I'm sure. The important thing is that we have enjoyed ourselves. Reading through this introduction I see I have used the word 'pleasure' three times plus 'enjoy' and 'delight'. Isn't that what we all feel about this craft and about all that lovely fabric waiting to be used?

Layer-Cake Quilts

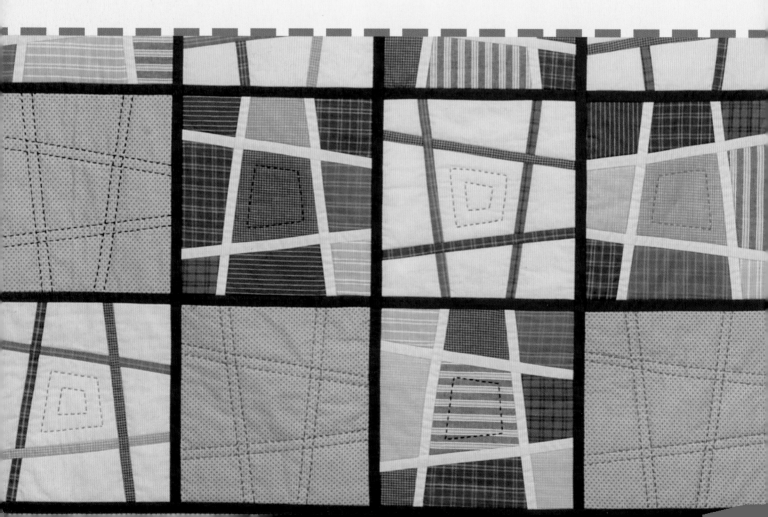

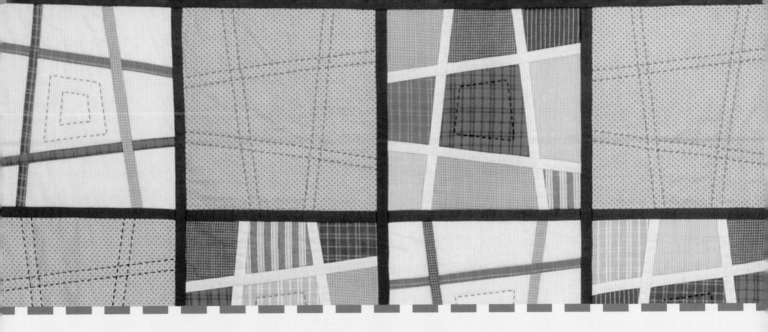

Quilters can seldom resist a pile of different fabrics carefully chosen to look good together and tied with ribbon or string in a seductive parcel. We buy them, admire them, but find it hard to break up the pile as it is the relationship between one fabric and its neighbour that pleases us. Once a piece is removed, it never seems to have quite the same magic. Well, with layer-cake quilts you can build on this pleasure: several squares of fabric are layered and then cut into wedges, just like cutting the slices of a layer-cake.

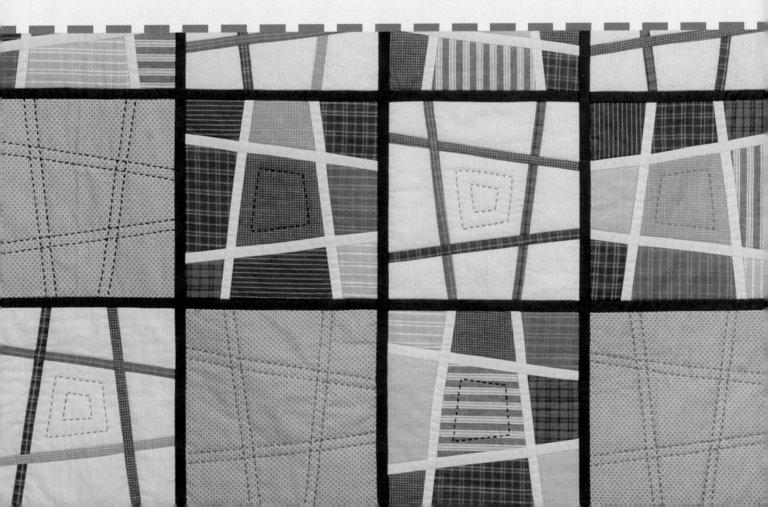

Spinning Pinwheels

This Spinning Pinwheel block creates a good sense of movement in a quilt and allows for either subtle or dramatic colour combinations. The fanned shape of the block is perfect for assessing how a group of fabrics work together and is very satisfying visually. The Subtle Spin quilt opposite is made from eight toning fabrics for the pinwheel blocks and two background fabrics used alternately in the blocks. The cutting for all the blocks is done at the same time. Each block looks different because the pieces are rearranged, although the step-by-step stages of construction are the same each time. The blocks are separated with sashing strips and a final 4in (10cm) border added. Sue Fitzgerald used the Spinning Pinwheel block to produce a lovely quilt in very different colours – see Blue-and-White Delight on page 15.

Subtle Spin

Finished block size 10in x 10in (25.3cm x 25.3cm)
Finished quilt size 55½in x 55½in (141cm x 141cm)

THE QUILT STORY

Every year fabric designers bring out a new range of fabrics, often in a co-ordinating set of colours. I bought assorted half yards of a truly delectable collection designed by Robyn Pandolph, all soft greens and pinks. Two years later when I finally found a project to suit it there wasn't a piece to be found anywhere to supplement my inadequate stash. Trawling through quilt shops and students' own fabrics, I finally acquired enough extra fabric to make the quilt. The moral of this story is: assume that when you buy from a new and probably temporary fabric range that you will finally want to use it in a decent-sized quilt. You need six yards in total for this quilt, not six half-yard pieces. . .

FABRIC REQUIREMENTS

◆ Pinwheel block fabrics: two squares each of eight fabrics, each cut 9in x 9in (22.8cm x 22.8cm).

◆ Background fabrics: 30in (76.2cm) each of two different fabrics each 42in–44in (106.7cm–111.8cm) wide.

◆ Sashing: 1yd (1m) of fabric plus 6in (15.2cm) of another fabric 42in–44in (106.7cm–111.8cm) wide for the contrast cornerstones.

◆ Border: 30in (76.2cm) of fabric 42in–44in (106.7cm–111.8cm) wide.

◆ Binding: 15in (38cm) of fabric 42in–44in (106.6cm–111.7cm) wide.

◆ Wadding and backing fabric: at least 2in (5cm) larger than finished quilt size.

Much time is saved on this quilt by eight layers of fabric being cut at the same time. The squares are then cut into wedges, each of which is used to make a block.

This quilt is a favourite of mine as I love the soft colours. I quilted it to death by hand over one summer – an excuse to sit in the sun and sew.

Construction

This technique makes eight blocks from the initial eight squares of pinwheel fabrics, so start by cutting and making the first eight blocks, and then repeat the process to make the second set of eight blocks.

CUTTING THE SQUARES

1 From each of the chosen pinwheel fabrics cut two squares, each 9in x 9in (22.7cm x 22.7cm). Set one square of each fabric aside to be used later in the second set of blocks. Take one square of each fabric and arrange them in a sequence that pleases you. Remember that the last fabric will link up with the first fabric in this pinwheel design. Note the order of the fabrics on a piece of paper and number each one.

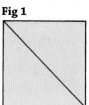

Cutting through eight layers at once sounds great, but accuracy can suffer as the fabric shifts a little with each cut. Instead, make two piles each with just four layers of fabric and reassemble into one pile after cutting.

2 Place the fabric squares numbered 1–4 on top of each other with 1 at the top and 4 at the bottom, all right side *upwards*. Line up the cut edges of the squares exactly. Use a rotary cutter and ruler to cut the squares diagonally from corner to corner (Fig 1). Repeat this from the other corner to corner diagonally (Fig 2).

Fig 1 **Fig 2**

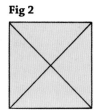

3 Without moving the layers of fabric, place the ruler horizontally across the centre of the fabric and the bottom edge of the fabric matching the 4½in marking on the ruler (Fig 3). Cut across the fabric squares.

Fig 3

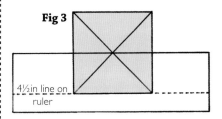

4½in line on ruler

4 Lift the ruler without disturbing the piles of fabric and place it vertically down the centre of the fabric with the left-hand edge of fabric matching the 4½in marking on the ruler (Fig 4). Left-handers should work from the right-hand side of the fabric. Cut through the fabric squares vertically. The four layers are now cut into eight triangles (Fig 5).

Fig 4

4½in line on ruler

Fig 5

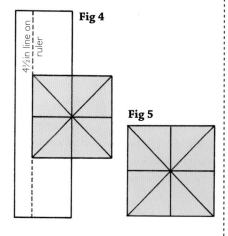

5 Repeat this with the squares of fabric numbered 5–8, with fabric 5 at the top and 8 at the bottom of the pile. Carefully place the first set of cut squares on top of the new set so that the order of fabrics goes in sequence from 1 at the top to 8 on the bottom.

The wedges of fabric will be used one at a time to make a block from each. This may take longer than planned (life gets in the way sometimes), so keep the cut layer-cake of fabrics in a tray or box so they stay in their neat wedges ready for use.

Arranging the pieces

6 Pick up the pile of triangles marked A in Fig 6. Arrange them in a cut square, starting with the top fabric 1 in position A and working round clockwise to finish with fabric 8 (Fig 7).

Fig 6   **Fig 7**

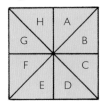

7 Turn pieces 1, 3, 5 and 7 to make the arrangement shown in Fig 8.

Fig 8

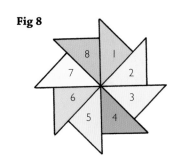

Making the block

8 From each of the two background fabrics cut four squares measuring 9in x 9in (22.7cm x 22.7cm) and thirty-two strips measuring 2in x 6¼in (5cm x 15.8cm). Cut each fabric square into eight pieces like the pinwheel fabrics in Fig 5.

9 Now take the pinwheel triangle numbered 2 in Fig 8 and place the triangle on a cut strip of background fabric with *right sides facing* as in Fig 9. The square corner of the triangle should match the top corner of the strip. Pin and stitch the triangle to the strip with the usual ¼in (6mm) seam allowance (Fig 10). Press the triangle out from the strip, ironing from the front of the work (Fig 11). Press the seam towards the triangle.

Fig 9
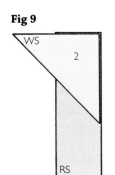

Fig 10
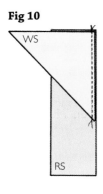

Fig 11
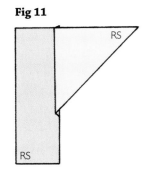

> Each triangle should always be placed in the same position as in Fig 9. Don't try to remember – check with the diagram!

Trimming the triangles

10 Use a rotary cutter and ruler to trim the strip to match the edge of the triangle. Place a square ruler on to the fabric, matching the fabric edges of the triangle with the edges of the ruler (Fig 12). Trim off the overhanging strip of background fabric along the edge of the ruler to make a pieced triangle, as shown in Fig 13.

Fig 12
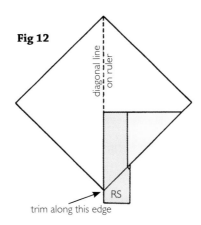
trim along this edge

Fig 13
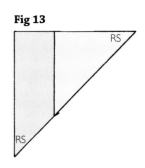

11 Place the pieced triangle back in the block (Fig 14). Repeat this process with triangles 4, 6 and 8. Place them back in the design (Fig 15).

Fig 14
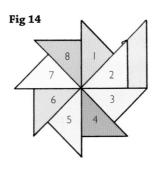

Fig 15
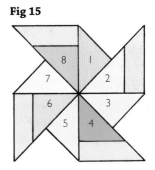

12 Take triangle 1 from the design. Arrange it with a triangle of background fabric as in Fig 16, with the square corners positioned as shown. Pin and stitch the two triangles together. Press the seam towards triangle 1, ironing from the front of the work (Fig 17).

Fig 16
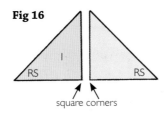
square corners

Fig 17
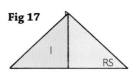

> Always place the triangle of background fabric on the right-hand side, because if you switch the triangles over they will not fit into the pinwheel design.

13 Place the joined triangles back in the block (Fig 18). Repeat this process with triangles 3, 5 and 7. Place them back in the design (Fig 19).

Fig 18

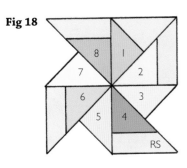

Fig 19

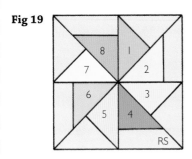

14 Take pieces 1 and 2. These need to be joined together along the diagonal seams (Fig 20). Pin and stitch the two pieces together, taking care not to stretch the bias edges of the fabric as you stitch. Press the seam towards piece 1. Repeat this to join pieces 3 and 4, then pieces 5 and 6 and then 7 and 8.

Fig 20

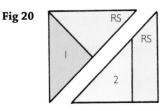

15 Trim the squares, if necessary, to exactly 5½in x 5½in (13.8cm x 13.8cm) and arrange them back into the Pinwheel block as in Fig 19.

Trimming the squares at this stage is really helpful as they will fit together more easily into the final block. Use a square ruler and match the diagonal line on the ruler with the diagonal seam on the fabric square when you trim.

Joining the block

16 Pin and stitch the top two squares together, matching seams carefully. Press the seam to the left, ironing from the front (Fig 21).

Fig 21

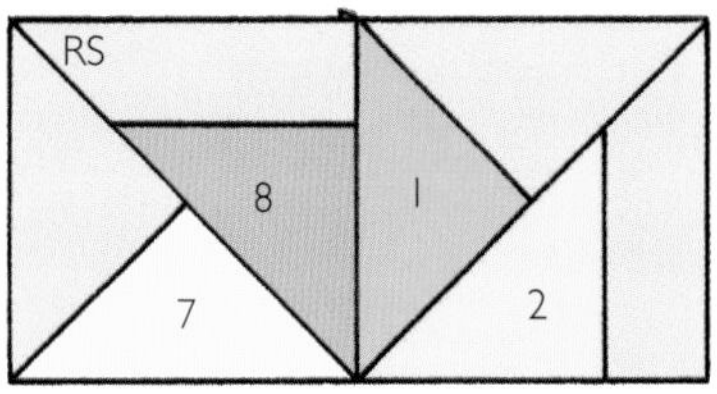

17 Pin and stitch the bottom two squares together. Press the seam to the right (Fig 22). Finally, join the two halves together, matching the centre seams carefully. Press the final long seam to one side. The remaining blocks can be arranged as block 1, or varied as described in the panel, right.

Fig 22

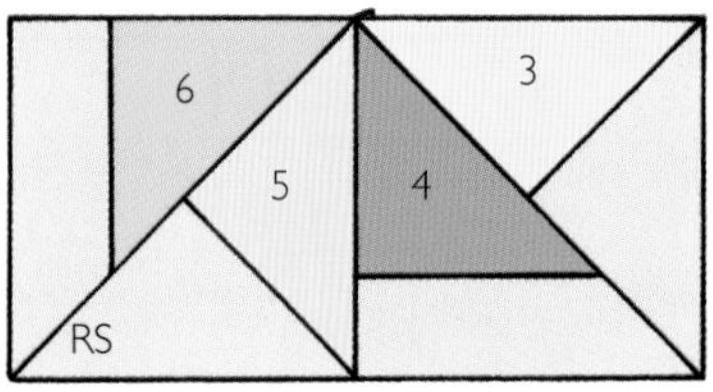

Making the second set of blocks

Repeat the block-making process to make another eight blocks, using the second set of eight fabric squares and the four squares and thirty-two strips of the second background fabric.

VARYING THE BLOCKS

You could repeat block 1 for the whole quilt or vary the spinning pinwheel colour layout so there are eight different blocks, as follows.

Block 2: pick up the pile of triangles marked B in Fig 6. Arrange them in a cut square, beginning with the top fabric 1 in position B in Fig 6 and working round clockwise to finish with fabric 8 (Fig 23). Once the fabrics are in position ignore their numbers and just follow the instructions as for block 1. All the fabrics will have shifted round one place in the circular design, which gives a very different effect.

Fig 23

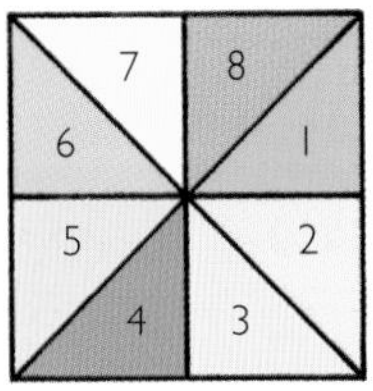

Block 3: pick up the pile of triangles marked C in Fig 6. Arrange them in the cut square beginning with the top fabric 1 in position C in Fig 6 and work round clockwise as before. Again, follow the instructions for block 1 using this new arrangement of triangles.

Block 4: use the triangles marked D in Fig 6 and lay them out with fabric 1 in position D in Fig 6, working round clockwise as before.

Block 5: use the triangles marked E in Fig 6 and lay them out with fabric 1 in position E in Fig 6, working round clockwise as before.

Block 6 starts at F, block 7 at G and block 8 at H. The completed blocks will now all have a different layout.

12   Spinning Pinwheels

L A Y E R - C A K E   Q U I L T S

SASHING THE BLOCKS

The sixteen blocks are sashed with pieced cornerstones that echo the pinwheel design of the block (Fig 24).

Fig 24

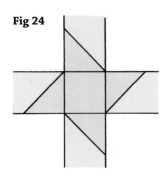

1 Arrange the sixteen blocks in four rows of four blocks (Fig 25).

Fig 25

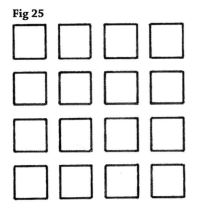

2 From the sashing fabric cut twenty-four strips each measuring 2in x 10½in (5cm x 26.6cm). From the fabric for the cornerstones cut forty-five squares each 2in x 2in (5cm x 5cm).

3 Pin a square of cornerstone fabric at one end of twelve of the cut sashing strips. Stitch diagonally across the square as in Fig 26.

Fig 26

The cornerstones must *always* be stitched in the same direction as shown in Fig 26.

4 Trim both fabrics ¼in (6mm) beyond the stitched line (Fig 27). Press the cornerstone piece away from the strip, ironing from the front (Fig 28).

Fig 27   **Fig 28**

Fig 29

5 In the same way, pin and stitch a square of cornerstone fabric to *both* ends of the other twelve sashing strips. Trim and press as before (Fig 29).

6 Pin and stitch three of the single-cornerstone sashing strips between the top row of blocks (Fig 30). Press the seams towards the sashing.

Fig 30

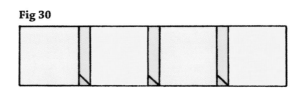

7 Repeat this for the bottom row of blocks, turning this row of blocks through 180 degrees once the cornerstones have been added.

8 Pin and stitch three double-cornerstone sashing strips between the blocks of both row 2 and row 3 (Fig 31).

Fig 31

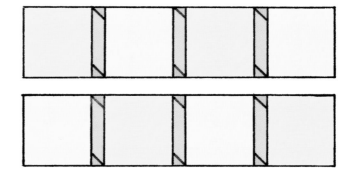

9 Join two single-cornerstone sashing strips and two double-cornerstone sashing strips together with three squares of cornerstone fabric as in Fig 32. Make two more joined strips like this.

Fig 32

10 Pin and stitch the three long joined strips between the rows of blocks, matching all the seams carefully (Fig 33). Press the seams towards the sashing.

Fig 33

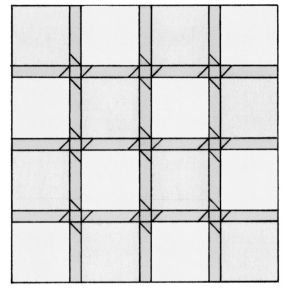

ADDING THE BORDERS

I framed the quilt with a border of sashing fabric cut 2½in (6.2cm) wide (finished width 2in/5cm). A second wider border was made from one of the pinwheel fabrics cut 4in (10cm) wide. (See Bordering a Quilt page 128.)

QUILTING

Each block was quilted by hand in the design shown in Fig 34. The sashing was quilted ¼in (6mm) away from the seams in the traditional way. The wide border has a design of triangles quilted on it (Fig 35). The quilt is bound in a dark green fabric that was also one of the pinwheel fabrics.

Fig 34

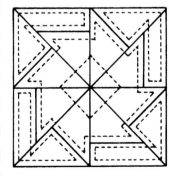

Fig 35

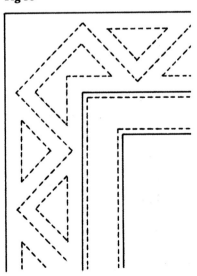

MAKING A LARGER QUILT

To make a single bed quilt 65½in x 90in (166.3cm x 228.5cm) like Sue Fitzgerald's (opposite), the number of blocks must be increased, from four rows with four blocks in each row (sixteen blocks in total) to seven rows with five blocks in each row (thirty-five blocks in total). This means making four sets of eight blocks (thirty-two blocks) plus three more blocks. To make another complete set of eight blocks is a waste of fabric and energy, so it's useful to know how to make individual blocks to make up the correct number for a quilt project. Also, if you want to make a really scrap quilt with every pinwheel block in different fabrics, this is the way to do it.

1 Choose eight different fabrics for the pinwheel. From each fabric cut one square 4½in x 4½in (11.3cm x 11.3cm). Cut each square in half diagonally (Fig 36) to give two identical triangles from each fabric. Use one set of triangles to make one block and the other set of triangles for a second block. If you only need one block, then save the second set of triangles for another project.

Fig 36

4½in

4½in (11.3cm)

2 From the chosen background fabric cut two squares each 4½in x 4½in (11.3cm x 11.3cm) and cut each square in half diagonally, to give four triangles, enough to make one block. From the background fabric cut four strips each 2in x 6¼in (5cm x 15.8cm). These will also make one block.

3 Now go back to the instructions on page 10 for arranging the pieces. Arrange the eight different triangles of fabric as in Fig 7 and then follow the instructions from steps 8–17 to make the block.

Blue-and-White Delight

Sue Fitzgerald made this beautifully fresh looking single-bed sized quilt in her favourite blue and white colour scheme using Spinning Pinwheel blocks but increasing the number of blocks to thirty-five – see the panel, left, for instructions on making a larger quilt.

" *I collect blue and white china and love using calico, so these colours really appealed to me. The rust-red accents, I felt, brought it to life. (Sue Fitzgerald)* "

Crazy Nine-Patch

You'll have fun using up some of your fabric stash on this quilt. Nine different squares of fabric are piled up and cut into pieces through all the layers at the same time. The pieces are then reassembled following a mathematical formula (which I've worked out for you) to make nine blocks, each with a different arrangement of all nine fabrics. The pieces of fabric in each block are joined with narrow contrasting sashing strips, while different coloured strips separate the finished blocks. Much time is saved by cutting all the blocks at the same time. Each block looks different from the others because the pieces are rearranged, although the stages of construction are the same each time.

Crazy in Amsterdam

Finished size of block 10½in x 10½in (26.7cm x 26.7cm)
Finished size of quilt 61in x 61in (155cm x 155cm)

THE QUILT STORY

The fabric collection I used for this quilt was bought in Amsterdam at vast expense and then hoarded for some years. There were only eight in the original group, so I had to search my stash to find an extra one that would join the team, plus a good background fabric and another for the sashing. I first made nine blocks using this layer-cake technique (blocks marked A in Fig 1). Then I found I hadn't enough of those nine fabrics to repeat the blocks, so I reversed the design, using my sashing fabric for the nine-patch blocks and an assortment of the nine original fabrics for the sashing strips (blocks B in Fig 1). Finally, I added eight plain squares of fabric, which were arranged between the others and quilted in the same nine-patch design (blocks C in Fig 1).

FABRIC REQUIREMENTS

◆ One fat quarter (either a ¼yd or ¼m) each of nine fabrics that will look good together in the first set of blocks (A). These will make the cut squares that are layered to make the design and are also used for sashing strips on the second set of nine-patch blocks (B).

◆ 1¾yd (1.6m) of a contrast fabric for narrow sashing in the first set of blocks (A) and the main fabric in the second set of blocks (B).

◆ 1½yd (1.37m) of a third fabric to make the C blocks (not pieced but quilted) and also for the final border.

◆ Wadding and backing fabric: at least 2in (5cm) larger than finished quilt size.

This quilt grows satisfyingly quickly as the nine A blocks are worked on at the same time. They all grow at the same rate and are finished simultaneously.

Fig 1

B	C	A	C	B
C	A	B	A	C
A	B	A	B	A
C	A	B	A	C
B	C	A	C	B

This crazy nine-patch quilt has a versatile design that will make good use of fabrics you already have, or give you an excuse to rush out and buy new stock . . .

Construction

MAKING SET A BLOCKS

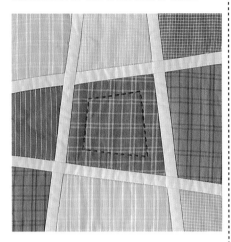

1 From each of the chosen nine fabrics cut a square measuring 11½in x 11½in (29.2cm x 29.2cm). For the sashing strips for this first set of blocks cut thirty-six strips each 1in x 12¼in (2.5cm x 31.1cm) from the chosen sashing fabric.

2 Cut nine squares of freezer paper about 1in (2.5cm) square. Number these 1–9. Place one roughly in the centre of each fabric square on the *right* side and fix it to the fabric by pressing with an iron on cool. Alternatively, fix with a safety pin.

! Do not use masking tape to fix the numbered labels on your fabric as it will leave a sticky deposit if the iron touches it when the block is being pressed during construction.

3 Pile up the marked fabric squares in order, with square 1 at the top and 9 at the bottom, matching up the edges of the squares carefully.

Making the wedge template

4 On a piece of graph paper draw a horizontal line 11½in (29.2cm) long. At the left end draw a vertical line downwards 4in (10.2cm) long. At the right end draw a vertical line downwards 2½in (6.4cm) long. Join these two lines from a to b to complete the wedge shape (Fig 2).

Fig 2

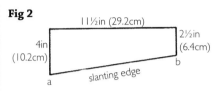

5 Cut out the wedge template carefully. Use masking tape to stick the template to the *underside* of a rotary ruler with right side *upwards* and the sloping edge a–b level with one long edge of the ruler (Fig 3).

Fig 3

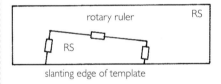

Cutting the squares

6 1st cut: place the ruler on the pile of fabric squares with the edges of the wedge template matching the edges of the fabric squares. Cut through all layers (Fig 4).

Fig 4

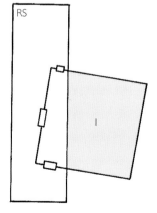

I used a large 60mm rotary cutter to cut through all nine layers in one go. If you find nine layers too many to cut accurately, separate the piles into 1–4 and 5–9. Cut each pile and reassemble the cut squares with square 1 at the top and 9 at the bottom. There are no prizes for cutting all the layers at once – accuracy and comfort of cutting with the rotary cutter are what matter.

Adding the sashing strip

7 Pin and stitch a 12¼in (31.1cm) length of 1in (2.5cm) wide sashing fabric to each of the smaller pieces of the cut squares (Fig 5). Press the seam towards the sashing, ironing from the front. Trim the ends of the sashing strips to match the edges of the fabric.

Fig 5

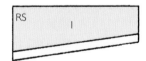

8 Place the smaller section of each block back with the larger sections in the correct order of layers to match the larger pieces as before.

9 Take the *marked* larger pieces 1 and 2 and move them to the bottom of the pile of marked pieces, still in the same order. This will leave the piece marked 3 at the top and piece 2 at the bottom. *Do not alter the smaller unmarked pieces* (Fig 6).

Fig 6

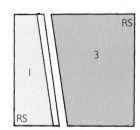

LAYER-CAKE QUILTS

10 Pin and stitch the two pieces of each block together, matching the cut ends of the sashing with the larger piece of fabric to make a square (Fig 7). Iron the seams towards the sashing, as before.

Fig 7

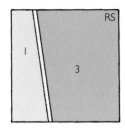

11 Pile the squares up in layers as before, still with piece number 1 at the top and number 9 at the bottom. Align the edges of each block carefully.

12 2nd cut: place the ruler on the blocks with the edges of the template matching the edges of the blocks as in Fig 8. Cut through all layers.

Fig 8

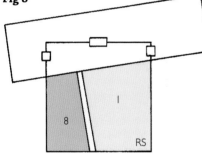

13 Pin and stitch a 12¼in (31.1cm) length of sashing to each of the smaller wedge shapes as before (Fig 9). This time do not trim the ends of the sashing level with the edges of the fabric after stitching. Press the seams towards the sashing, ironing from the front.

Fig 9

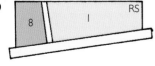

14 Place the smaller pieces back with their partners in the pile, with the piece marked 1 at the top as before and piece 9 at the bottom.

15 Take the large marked pieces 1–6 and move them to the bottom of the pile. It should now have piece 7 at the top and piece 6 at the bottom. *Do not alter the smaller unmarked pieces* (Fig 10).

Fig 10

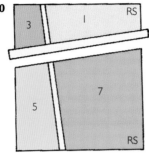

16 Stitch together the two sections of each layer to make squares as before, aligning the sashing on both pieces to form a 'crossroads' (Fig 11, plus see advice panel, right, Figs 12a, 12b and 13). Press the seam towards the sashing, ironing from the front. Trim the sashing to match the edges of the block and then pile up the blocks as before with piece number 1 at the top and piece 9 at the bottom.

Fig 11

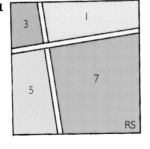

MATCHING SASHING STRIPS ON A SLANTING ANGLE

This can be tricky. First find the centre of the slanting edge on each piece by folding as in Figs 12a and 12b. Crease to mark each centre. Match the centre of the stitching line and pin the junction of the sashing with a horizontal pin (Fig 13). Open up the two pieces to check that the sashings are matched before pinning at right angles as usual along the fabric edges, matching the ends of each section of the block carefully.

Fig 12a

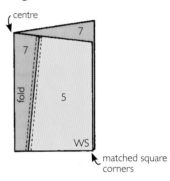

Fig 12b

Fig 13

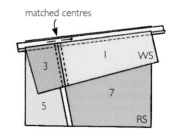

17 3rd cut: *before cutting*, remove the wedge template carefully from the ruler. *Turn it over* and stick it back to the underside of the ruler. This reverses the template for the remaining two cuts (Fig 14). Now use the template on the ruler to cut the blocks as shown in Fig 15.

Fig 14

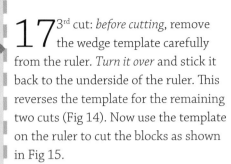

Fig 15

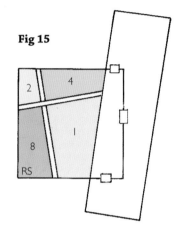

18 Pin and stitch a length of sashing to the smaller sections of the block as before. Place these back with their partners in the pile, keeping the blocks in order with piece 1 at the top and piece 9 at the bottom.

19 Move the large pieces marked 1–4 to the bottom of the pile, leaving piece 5 on the top and piece 4 at the bottom. *Do not alter the smaller pieces.*

20 Join the two cut sections of each block with the sashing to make squares as before (Fig 16).

Fig 16

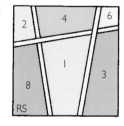

Match the sashing crossroads as carefully as possible (see advice panel

and Figs 12a, 12b and 13 on previous page). Press the seams towards the sashing and then trim the ends of the sashing strips level with the edges of the block. Now pile up the blocks as usual with the marked piece 1 on the top and piece 9 on the bottom.

21 4th cut: use the wedge template on the ruler to make the last cut (Fig 17).

Fig 17

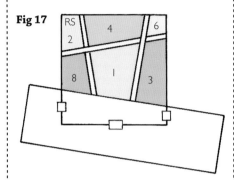

22 Pin and stitch a sashing strip to the smaller section of each block. Press towards the sashing. Reassemble the blocks in order with the marked piece 1 on the top and piece 9 on the bottom.

23 Move the large pieces marked 1–3 to the bottom of the pile, leaving piece 4 on the top and piece 3 on the bottom. *Do not alter the smaller pieces.*

24 Join the two parts of each block together with sashing as before. This time there will be two crossroads of sashing to be aligned, so match them carefully before stitching. Press from the front as usual and trim the ends of the sashing strips level with the sides of the block (Fig 18).

Fig 18

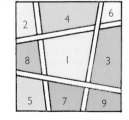

25 Trim the finished blocks to measure 11in x 11in (27.9cm x 27.9cm).

MAKING SET B BLOCKS

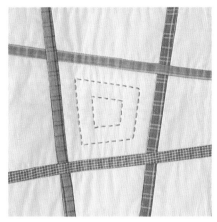

1 Here only eight blocks need to be made and the fabrics are reversed, so the sashing fabric from Set A is used for the pile of eight squares and some or all of the main fabrics from Set A become the sashing strips in Set B. From the fabric used as the sashing in the A blocks cut eight squares, each measuring 11½in x 11½in (29.2cm x 29.2cm) as before. These do not have to be numbered as they are all from the same fabric. For the sashing cut thirty-two strips from any or all of the nine fabrics used for the starting squares for the A blocks, each strip 1in x 12¼in (2.5cm x 31.1cm).

2 Remove the wedge template from the ruler, *turn it over* and stick it back to the underside of the ruler. This is the starting position it was in for cutting the blocks in Set A (see Fig 3 on page 18).

3 Pile up the eight cut squares, matching the edges carefully. Now follow the instructions given in steps 6–25 for making the Set A blocks.

When making the B blocks, there is no need to rearrange the layers at any time as they are all the same fabric. So to save time, just cut, add the sashing strips, join together and pile up ready for the next cut. Don't forget to turn the wedge template over after the first two cuts.

LAYER-CAKE QUILTS

MAKING SET C BLOCKS

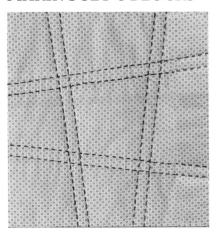

From the chosen fabric cut eight squares each measuring 11in x 11in (27.9cm x 27.9cm) to match the trimmed blocks from Sets A and B. Use the wedge template as a guide to mark quilting lines in the same design as the pieced blocks (Fig 19).

Fig 19

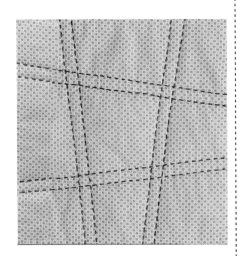

quilting lines

The C blocks can be turned to link up the narrow sashing in adjacent blocks.

JOINING ALL THE BLOCKS

1 Arrange the twenty-five blocks to make your chosen design, five rows of five blocks (see Fig 1 on page 16).

2 From the fabric chosen to act as sashing between the completed blocks cut twenty strips each 1in x 11in (2.5cm x 27.9cm). Pin and stitch a sashing strip between the blocks in each row (Fig 20). Press the seams towards the sashing, ironing from the front.

When you are arranging all of your blocks, remember that the individual blocks can be rotated in any direction to create different effects, so experiment before deciding on the final layout.

Fig 20

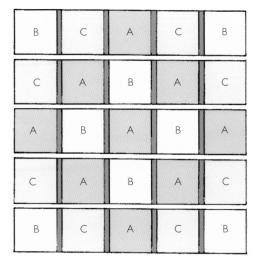

3 From the sashing fabric cut four strips each measuring 1in x 53in (2.5cm x 134.6cm). Pin and stitch these strips between the five rows of blocks (Fig 21). Press the seams towards the sashing.

Fig 21

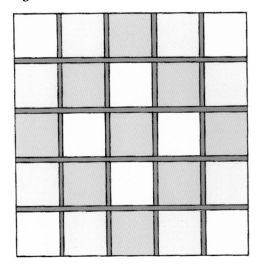

ADDING THE BORDER

1 From the sashing fabric used between the blocks cut the following:

two strips 1in x 53in (2.5cm x 134.6cm);
two strips 1in x 61in (2.5cm x 154.9cm) and
two strips 1in x 4in (2.5cm x 10.2cm).
From the border fabric cut four strips each
4in x 53in (10.2cm x 134.6cm) and
four cornerstone squares 4in x 4in
(10.2cm x 10.2cm).

2 Join a cornerstone square of border fabric to either end of two of the long border strips with the 4in (10.2cm) lengths of sashing as in Fig 22. Press the seams into the sashing.

Fig 22

3 Pin and stitch one of the 53in (134.6cm) lengths of sashing to each of two lengths of border strip (Fig 23). Press the seams into the sashing.

Fig 23

4 Pin and stitch these to each side of the quilt (Fig 24). Press seams into the sashing.

Fig 24

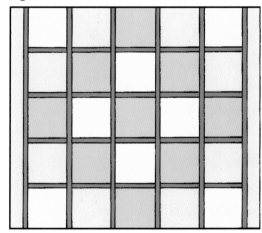

5 In the same way pin and stitch the remaining sashing to the border strips with the cornerstones (Fig 25).

Fig 25

6 Stitch these to the top and bottom of the quilt, matching the 'crossroads' of sashing strips at the cornerstones carefully (Fig 26).

Fig 26

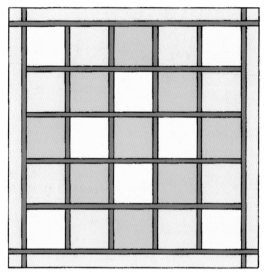

QUILTING

I machine quilted very closely to the sashing strips throughout the quilt in matching thread. I used thick perlé thread to hand quilt in a larger stitch in the centre block of each of the pieced blocks and also to create the nine-patch design on the plain squares (Fig 27). The final binding is in the same fabric used to sash between the blocks.

Fig 27

A block

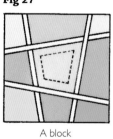

B block

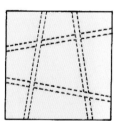

C block

French Connection

Shirley Prescott made this design into a single bed quilt by making two sets
of blocks in different red fabrics with white sashing and seventeen blocks with
white as the main fabric and red strips for the sashing – a total of thirty-five blocks.

> *I made this quilt for my step-granddaughter, Katy, for her 21st birthday. A limited set
> of colours made the geometric design quite striking. She must have liked the quilt as she
> took it off to France with her when she taught there for six months. (Shirley Prescott)*

Stitch-a-Strip

The strip-based quilts in this section are all vibrant and interesting designs and excellent for using up your scraps and leftovers, as well as for your precious collections. When using strips it may be possible to cut across the fabric giving strips as long as 44in (112cm) but many will be far too short. Strips cut down the fabric parallel to the woven selvedge will be much firmer. It is almost impossible to avoid cutting both types of strips when so many different fabrics are being used, so use the more stretchy strips with care, trying not to pull them when stitching. It may help to spray starch all the fabrics before cutting them into strips, which will help to keep the strips firmer.

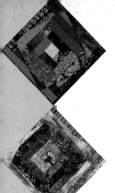

Tilted Log Cabin

This is a new slant (literally) on the ever-versatile Log Cabin. Each Log Cabin block is made and trimmed to an exact square. A triangular template is used to cut off the four corners of the block which are then moved to their opposite positions and re-stitched into place (see Fig 1 overleaf). This gives an interesting tilted look to the centre of the Log Cabin block while the corners stay square. Jean Campbell's queen-size quilt (Syncopation, opposite) accentuates the tilted angles by the use of bold contrasting colours, while Sue Fawcett's stunning lap quilt (Off-Beat Batik, overleaf) blends a fabulous range of batiks. Gill Shepherd took the technique further for her Tilting at Windmills quilt on page 33.

Syncopation

Finished block size 14in x 14in (35.5cm x 35.5cm)
Finished size of Syncopation 83in x 95½in (210.8cm x 242.6cm)
Finished size of Off-Beat Batik (overleaf) 46½in x 46½in (118.1cm x 118.1cm)

THE QUILT STORY

The principle of this tilted technique was outlined in an American magazine some while ago. I was intrigued and started to play with it to make it user-friendly for my students. Jean Campbell began her Syncopation quilt (opposite) on a one-day class for this technique, using just fabric from her stash and leftovers, but only after a really determined effort to finish up some of her UFOs (Un-Finished Objects) did she later develop a completed block into this queen-size quilt.

Sue Fawcett began Off-Beat Batik (overleaf) on her annual trip to Suffolk for a summer school, using up some of her batik collection. Every block began with a centre square of a striking yellow flower print and then moved into purples on one side and greens on the other.

FABRIC REQUIREMENTS

This Log Cabin design needs two contrasting teams of fabric (A and B), which are stitched around a square of different fabric in each block centre. Sort through your stored fabrics and find as many as possible (at least six) that blend together for one team and another group for the opposing colour team.

◆ **For Syncopation**: about 3yd (3m) of each team of fabrics for the Log Cabin blocks plus ½yd (0.5m) for the centres.

◆ **Borders**: there are four – the first and last use fabric leftover from the Log Cabin blocks. The second border takes an extra ½yd (0.5m) of one of the red/purple fabrics. The third wide green border needs 1yd (1m) of fabric.

◆ **Binding**: an extra ½yd (0.5m) of one of the green fabrics.

◆ **For Off-Beat Batik**: about 1yd (1m) for each team of fabrics, plus a 9in (22.8cm) square of fabric to make all the centres of the blocks.

◆ **Border and binding**: another 1yd (1m) of fabric.

◆ **For both quilts**: wadding and backing fabric: at least 2in (5cm) larger than finished quilt size.

Make four Log Cabin blocks at the same time before cutting them up to make the tilted blocks.

" *I began this quilt in a class with Lynne ages ago. I went home inspired to make a full-size quilt but, of course, it was a couple of years later that I pulled it out of its bag and carried on from the three blocks that I had made earlier. (Jean Campbell)* "

Off-Beat Batik

Batiks are wonderful fabrics for patchwork. Each one has many varied patterns and colours swirling within the fabric, which provide lots of choices for patchwork layouts.

After selecting and cutting the strips from five pink/purple and five green/turquoise batik fabrics plus squares with a cheeky gold daisy peeping out, I assembled the Log Cabin blocks using the fabrics in rotation. This resulted in five different blocks and four duplicates. The quilting pattern evolved from the shapes created by the blocks and was continued out to the edge of the borders. (Sue Fawcett)

Construction

The instructions that follow apply to making the Syncopation and Off-Beat Batik quilts. If you are confident about making the classic Log Cabin block, then start reading from step 12 on page 31. If you require more help, start from step 1 below and refer to Fig 2.

MAKING THE LOG CABIN BLOCKS

1 Cut strips 2in (5cm) wide from all the fabrics in both colour teams. Cut pieces for the centre squares each 2½in x 2½in (6.3cm x 6.3cm). The strips should be used as randomly as possible within each colour team to give a scrap effect. The block has four complete rounds of strips built out from the centre square (Fig 2). Each block needs to measure

Fig 1

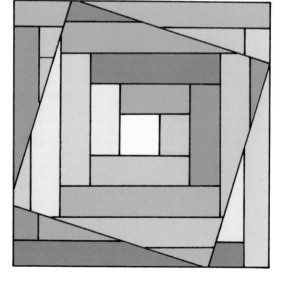

Strips cut in the same direction as the selvedge will be far less stretchy and easier to handle than strips cut across the fabric from selvedge to selvedge. If you have to use strips cut across the fabric, do not pull on them as you stitch, to avoid stretching. Alternatively, spray starch your fabrics before you cut the strips, which will keep them firmer.

exactly 14in x 14in (35.5cm x 35.5cm) before the corners are cut off and re-positioned. The block in Fig 2 should measure ½in (1.2cm) more than this and will need to be trimmed to the right size before cutting the corners.

2 Make four blocks at once using the following speedy method. Cut four squares of fabric for the centres each 2½in x 2½in (6.3cm x 6.3cm).

3 Stick a small square of masking tape on to the back of one of the centre squares, avoiding the ¼in (6mm) seam allowance. Label the tape with numbers 1, 2, 3 and 4 as in Fig 3. The numbers give a guide to where each strip will be stitched.

Fig 2

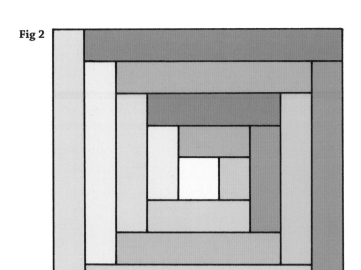

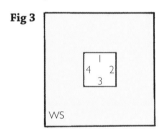

Fig 3

4 Take a cut strip from team A fabrics at least 12in (30.5cm) long. Place it right side *up* on the machine in the correct position for a ¼in (6mm) seam to be sewn. Lower the pressure foot and wind the needle down into the fabric. Now the pressure foot can be lifted and the centre squares added without the first strip slipping out of position.

5 Place the first centre square right side *down* on the strip with side 1 on the masking tape as the edge to be stitched. Using a short stitch and a ¼in (6mm) seam, sew the centre square on to the strip. Sew onwards a few stitches and place a second square in position, then add the third and fourth squares in the same way (Fig 4).

Fig 4

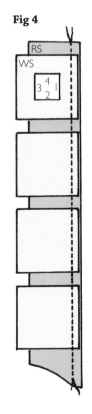

6 Remove the strip from the machine and carefully trim it to match the centre squares exactly (Fig 5). Finger-press the seams away from the centre squares (Fig 6).

Fig 5

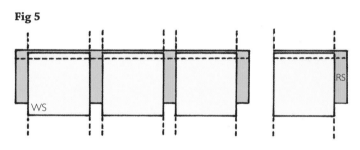

Fig 6

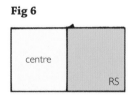

7 In building up the Log Cabin rounds of strips, each colour team of fabrics is used twice, making an L shape. This can be of the same fabric or a different fabric from the team – your choice. So put the second fabric strip (either the same fabric or another from team A) on the sewing machine again, right side *up* and move the needle down into the fabric. Take the original block with its piece of masking tape and place it right side *down* on the strip with side 2 at the edge to be stitched (Fig 7). Sew down this edge and place the second block on the strip in the same way. The first block is your model and the next three blocks must follow the same arrangement as they are positioned on the

Fig 7

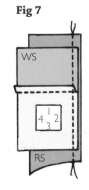

Tilted Log Cabin

strip. Stitch block 2 and add the third and fourth blocks to match (Fig 8).

Fig 8

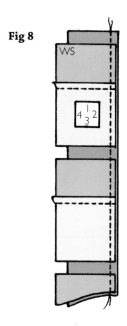

Now trim the strip either side of the blocks to match exactly the edges of the four blocks (Fig 9), then finger-press the seams away from the centre square (Fig 10).

Fig 9

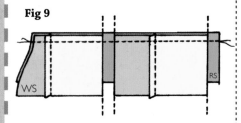

Fig 10

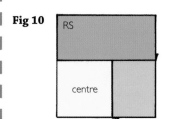

8 Having stitched on two strips from the first team of fabrics (A), take a strip of fabric from team B and place it on the machine again, right side *up* with the needle wound down into it. Position the original block right side *down* with side 3 on the masking tape

at the sewing edge (Fig 11). Sew down this edge and add the remaining three blocks to match the first (Fig 12).

Fig 11

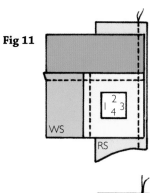

Fig 12

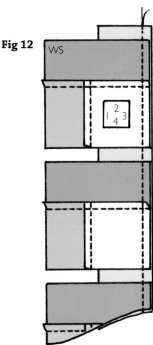

Trim the strips to match each block and finger-press the seams away from the centre (Fig 13).

Fig 13

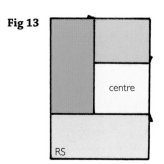

9 Using another strip of fabric from team B, either the same as before or a different fabric from the team (remember, always use each team *twice* to make an L shape), follow the same procedure, stitching side 4 of each block on to the strip. You now have a complete round of strips surrounding the centre square (Fig 14).

Fig 14

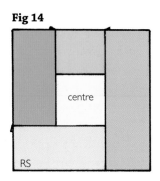

Once the block has got this far there is a quick way to see at a glance which side of the block is the next one to be stitched. Look at the block and find the edge that has two seams along it – this is the side to be stitched next (Fig 15).

Fig 15

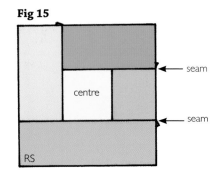

As you stitch check that the strip will be long enough for the next block to be stitched to it. If too short, just substitute another strip from any fabric from the team for the remaining blocks to be stitched on to.

10 Continue to build up the block, referring to the masking tape square to check that sides 1 and 2 always have team A fabrics against them, while sides 3 and 4 have team B fabrics against them. Remember to use strips from each team *twice* to make the L shape.

11 When four rounds of strips have been joined to all four blocks, check with Fig 2 (page 29) that the design is correct. Press each block from the front, pressing all the seams out from the centre towards the edges of the block.

12 For those of you confident enough to make Log Cabin blocks without the previous detailed instructions, start from here by measuring the completed block – it should be about 14½in x 14½in (36.8cm x 36.8cm) before trimming. Trim each block on all sides to exactly 14in x 14in (35.5cm x 35.5cm).

13 Now make more blocks in the same arrangement of strips as in Fig 2. Thirty blocks are needed for the Syncopation quilt on page 27. Nine blocks are needed for the Off-Beat Batik quilt on page 28. Do not worry too much if the final round of strips varies in width because of the trimming – this won't be noticeable once the blocks are cut up and tilted.

Making the triangular template

14 On a piece of graph paper draw a horizontal line 11in (27.9cm) long. At the left end draw a vertical line upwards 3½in (8.9cm). Join these two lines from a to b (Fig 16) to complete the triangle.

Fig 16

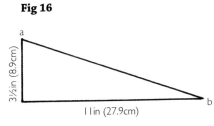

15 Cut out the triangle template carefully. Use masking tape to stick the template to the *underside* of a rotary ruler with right side *upwards* and the sloping edge a–b level with one long edge of the ruler (Fig 17).

Fig 17

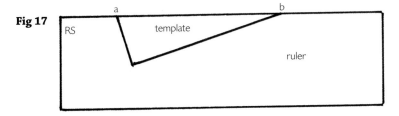

Cutting the blocks

16 Lay a Log Cabin block right side up on a cutting mat. Place the ruler over the block so that the template triangle is positioned exactly over one corner of the block. Cut along the edge of the ruler through the fabric block (Fig 18).

Fig 18

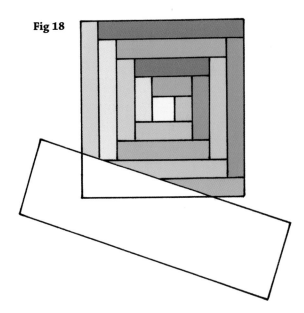

17 Repeat this on the *opposite* corner of the block. Finally, repeat this cut on the remaining two corners (Fig 19).

Fig 19

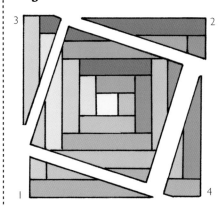

Only the first pair of opposite triangles of fabric cut from the block are completely triangular in shape. The other two have the last ½in (1.2cm) of the sharp point (b) missing and a small piece from the other corner (a) – see Fig 20.

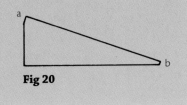

Fig 20

Tilted Log Cabin   31

18 Exchange corner 1 with its opposite corner 2 and exchange corner 3 with corner 4 (Fig 21).

Fig 21

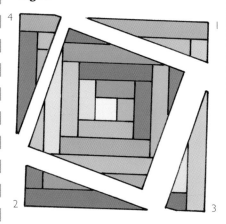

19 Pin and stitch corner 1 to the centre block with a ¼in (6mm) seam offset along the seamline at the wide-angled end and with an overhang at the sharp-angled end (Fig 22).

Fig 22

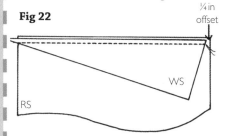

20 Pin and stitch the opposite corner 2 to the block in the same way. Press both corners back out from the centre block, ironing from the front of the work.

21 Pin and stitch corners 3 and 4 to the centre block. Both will have points missing from either end as Fig 20, so the wide-angled corner should be positioned as in Fig 23. The sharp corner at the other end of the stitching line will still overhang the block, but not as much as corners 1 and 2.

Fig 23

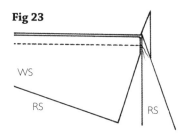

22 Press back stitched corners 3 and 4 from the block, ironing from the front of the work.

23 Repeat this process of cutting the corners, repositioning and re-stitching them on all blocks for the quilt, following steps 16–22 each time.

JOINING THE BLOCKS

1 When all the blocks are stitched, trim off as little as possible to straighten the edges. Each block should measure 13in x 13in (33cm x 33cm). If this is not the case, don't worry. Just trim all the blocks to the same size as each other so they will be easy to join. The tilted corners of the centre block may be lost in the trimming but they will all disappear into the seams anyway when the blocks are joined. The eye does not notice this; in fact it assumes the corners are there and enjoys the dancing effect of the tilted blocks.

2 Take the trimmed blocks and arrange them in a design that pleases you. Sue's Off-Beat Batik quilt (page 28) has nine blocks – three rows with three blocks in each row. You may choose, as Sue did, to turn every other block through 90 degrees so that the colours in each corner alternate.

Jean's Syncopation quilt (page 27) has six rows of blocks with five blocks in each row. Jean made half her blocks tilting to one side and the other half tilting in the other direction. This was a direct result of a mistake – how often innovative design is the outcome of going wrong with the original pattern! She left the project for some time while doing other things and when she took it up again she stuck the triangle template on to her ruler upside down, so that when she cut the triangles off her blocks they were a mirror-image of the ones she had already done. Hastily she re-thought her design and made fifteen blocks as in my instructions and fifteen blocks as a reverse image – triumph snatched from disaster.

3 Start joining the blocks by pinning and stitching the top row of blocks together. Press the seams to one side, ironing from the front of the work.

4 Pin and stitch the second row of blocks together. Press the seams in the *opposite* direction to row 1, ironing from the front. Continue to pin and stitch each row, pressing seams in alternate directions to help lock them.

5 Join the rows together, matching seams carefully. Press seams to one side from the front.

ADDING THE BORDERS

Jean's quilt had a series of borders to frame the blocks and make the quilt big enough for a bed. The first was made from strips of dark red fabrics used in her blocks cut 3in (7.6cm) wide, finishing 2½in (6.3cm) wide. The second border was another dark red fabric cut 2½in (6.3cm) wide, finishing 2in (5cm) wide. A wide green border was next, cut 4½in (11cm), finishing 4in (10cm) wide. The final border was made from leftover strips of green fabrics used in the blocks, each cut 2in (5cm) wide, finishing 1½in (3.8cm) wide. The quilt was bound in another green fabric used in the blocks.

Sue's small quilt was framed and bound in a contrasting fabric cut 4½in (11.4cm) wide, finishing 4in (10cm).

QUILTING

Jean had her quilt machine-quilted with a long-arm machine by Jan Chandler, an expert in this field, and was really pleased with the result.

Sue machined her quilt with a variegated metallic thread, stitching just in the seam lines of each Log Cabin block. She continued the quilting into the dark border in the same design as the pieced blocks. The metallic thread shimmers as it catches the light and is really effective.

Tilting at Windmills

Gill Shepherd made this interesting quilt using the Tilted Log Cabin block.
She continued to use the tilting technique with the pieced strip borders
to create a very striking and effective look to her quilt.

*'Please don't give me a quilt,' pleaded my sister – until she saw this
one that I'd made from my collection of scraps of Liberty fabrics.
'I like that one!' she said, so it's hers. (Gill Shepherd)*

Bargello

It is only recently that the term Bargello has been used in association with patchwork. Traditionally it is the name for Florentine canvas embroidery where parallel vertical stitches are worked in subtle shadings of wool. Each line of stitches is worked in a different shade from the one before to make curves or flame-like points. The principle of this applied to patchwork creates some fascinating effects. The Crimson Wave lap quilt (opposite) uses the technique in a 16in x 15¾in (40.6cm x 40cm) block, which is repeated four times and joined to make the quilt. Three borders frame the quilt. The inner and final border and binding are plain red to calm the busy centre area. The middle border is made from leftover strips of the red-based fabrics used in the main design.

Crimson Wave

Finished block size 16in x 15¾in (40.6cm x 40cm)
Finished quilt size 48in x 47in (119cm x 122cm)

THE QUILT STORY

Yvonne Dawson brought her Bargello lap quilt to a weekend workshop in an unfinished form, saying it had been at that stage for several years and she needed to get it finished. It looked so good once it was finished I suggested it could be included in this book, if I could work out some instructions for it. 'You should be able to', she replied. 'It was a project in a magazine, and you wrote it'.

When choosing fabrics, the jump from one colour to another can be bridged by using a linking fabric with both colours in it. Select fabrics you think might be useful and arrange them side by side and overlapping, to give an idea of how a small amount relates to its neighbour. Do not limit yourself to eight to start with: once they are arranged you can weed out the less essential. Both prints and plains are fine to use, even very large prints as these add interest and become abstract when cut up. Move the fabrics around and aim for gentle shading rather than sharp contrasts.

FABRIC REQUIREMENTS

Eight fabrics are needed for the design (see Fig 1 overleaf), shaded from light to dark. Yvonne started with a white fabric with red patterning and gradually moved through deeper red patterns. She used one rogue fabric with green in it as well as red, to give an extra buzz to the design.

◆ Bargello patchwork: 13in (33cm) each of eight fabrics 42in–44in wide (106.7cm x 111.8cm) – see advice, left.

◆ Borders and binding: 1yd (1m) of fabric.

◆ Wadding and backing fabric: at least 2in (5cm) larger than finished quilt size.

The complex-looking design is easily made from strips of different fabrics stitched together before being cut into pieces and rearranged.

"Having acquired lots of red fabrics over the years I decided they had to be used. I found them difficult to work with at first as they are not my usual choice of colours but was delighted with the result. (Yvonne Dawson)"

STITCH-A-STRIP

Construction

MAKING A BARGELLO BLOCK

1 Make one Bargello block at a time (Fig 1). From each of the eight chosen fabrics cut two strips each 1½in (3.8cm) wide and about 28in (71.1cm) long.

Fig 1

> If you cannot get strips as long as 28in (71.1cm) just join two shorter strips together and press the seam open. When cutting the pieces from the joined strips later, just avoid cutting a piece with this seam in it – jump over the seam and start cutting again.

2 Arrange the strips in the order that you intend using them. From leftover scraps cut a small piece from each fabric (about 1in /2.5cm square) and stick them vertically on a piece of paper or card. Number each fabric as shown in Fig 2 – you will need to refer to this chart as you work.

Fig 2

3 Using a smaller stitch than for dressmaking (about two-thirds of the size) and a ¼in (6mm) seam, stitch together one strip each of the eight fabrics in the chosen order. Alternate the direction of stitching with each strip (see arrows in Fig 3), as this helps to keep the band of strips flat. Do not press the band yet.

Fig 3

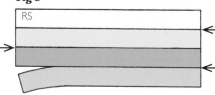

4 Repeat the process with the second set of strips. Check that both have their fabrics in the same sequence.

5 Join the two bands together to make a single band of sixteen strips, keeping the colours in the same repeat order (Fig 4).

Fig 4

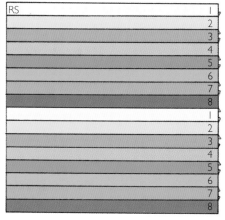

6 Press the seams in alternate directions (Fig 5) – see tip below.

Fig 5

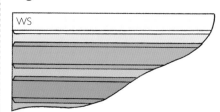

> Press lightly from the back to establish the directions of the seams. Then flip the piece over and press firmly from the front. Make sure the seams are pulled open without folds or the strip widths will not be accurate.

7 Place the piece on a flat surface and with the right side *upwards* as shown in Fig 4 bring the bottom strip (fabric 8) up so that it lies on the top strip (fabric 1) with right sides together and the long unstitched edges matching (Fig 6). Check that the piece is lying flat and not twisted, and then pin. It does not matter if the side edges do not match – just that both layers of fabric are lying flat.

STITCH-A-STRIP

Fig 6

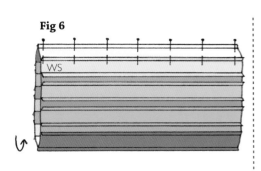

8 Now stitch the pinned seam to make a tube. Press the seam in whichever direction fits the alternating arrangement of seams in the rest of the band. Leave the tube with the seams on the *outside* as Fig 6.

Cutting the pieces

9 Place the tube of fabrics flat on a cutting mat, lining the top edges up with a horizontal marking on the board. Straighten one end, wasting as little fabric as possible. Now study the cutting chart in Fig 7 (bottom of page). The first column gives all the information for the first piece to be cut. The top line shows the width of the piece to be cut which is 1¼in (3.2cm). Cut the piece as in Fig 8.

Fig 8

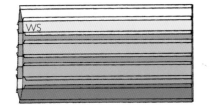

What you have at this stage is a loop. The two other rows in the chart column of Fig 7 tell you where the seam must be undone to convert the loop into a long piece. For the first piece the top fabric is no.8 and the bottom is no.7. They occur twice in the loop but just locate one pair and ignore the other. Hold fabric 8 in your left hand and fabric 7 in your right and undo the seam that joins them. Pin the piece on a board or lay it out on a clear surface with fabric 8 at the top and fabric 7 at the bottom (Fig 9). Tick the first column on the chart to show that you have dealt with that piece.

> ! It's all too easy to stitch the multi-fabric strips together in the wrong order, or to put a strip in upside down. Use a board to pin the pieces on and keep things in order. Pin each pieced strip on it as it is cut, checking with Fig 1 that the design is correct.

10 Cut piece 2, which is also 1¼in (3.2cm) wide. Find fabrics 7 and 6 next to each other in the loop. Hold fabric 7 in one hand and fabric 6 in the other hand and undo the seam that joins them. Place this second piece next to the first piece with fabric 7 at the top and fabric 6 at the bottom, working from left to right (Fig 10). Tick the second column on the chart in Fig 7 once you have done this.

Fig 9

Fig 10

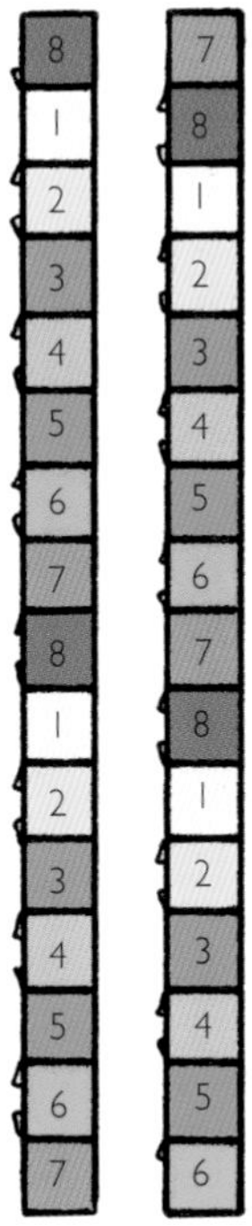

Fig 7

WIDTH OF STRIP	1¼in	1¼in	1½in	2½in	1½in	1¼in	1¼in	1in	¾in	¾in	¾in	1in	1¼in	1¼in	1½in	2½in	1½in	1¼in	1¼in
TOP FABRIC	8	7	6	5	6	7	8	1	2	3	2	1	8	7	6	5	6	7	8
BOTTOM FABRIC	7	6	5	4	5	6	7	8	1	2	1	8	7	6	5	4	5	6	7

11 Continue to cut each piece in turn, following the width measurements from the Fig 7 chart. The pattern of curves and steps develop as the pieces are unstitched and placed next to each other. The arrows on the chart show where the slope comes to a peak or dips to a valley. The slope descends through four pieces to a broad base and then climbs to a narrow peak in the centre of the block. It then descends and rises as a mirror image of the first half (see Fig 1). There should be a short section of the pieced tube of fabric left after all nineteen pieces have been cut. Set this aside for later, when an extra two strips will be cut from it.

✂

In the centre of the design are three strips that make the peak. These are cut ¾in (1.9cm) wide, finishing ¼in (6mm) wide after stitching. If this seems too fiddly, just increase the width of each cut strip from ¾in (1.9cm) to 1in (2.5cm), which means the three strips will be slightly wider.

Stitching the block

12 When all the pieces have been cut and arranged, begin pinning and stitching them together. Remove each strip from the board as it is pinned and stitched to its neighbour. Place the block back each time after a new strip is added and check it has been stitched correctly. To join, place the two strips right sides together and stitch lengthwise, matching seams carefully. The initial pressing of the seams in alternate directions means that the seams will lock together so you can stitch without pinning if you want to.

There are no rules: if you feel you need to pin each junction before you stitch, then do so. Take particular care to match seams where there are definite changes in colour as any inaccuracies will show up here. In other areas where the fabrics are more subtly shaded, a mismatched seam may not be noticeable at all – wait until the whole block is pieced before making a decision to re-stitch a seam, as you may well find that it has merged in with the design.

13 Once all the pieces are joined, the block needs to be pressed from the front with the long vertical seams pressed all to one side. Some of the pieces, especially the very narrow ones, will probably look uneven in width. Use a steam iron to get them pulled out as evenly as possible. Trim the top and bottom edges to straighten them but use the steam iron and some judicious pulling to get the sides straight.

Making the remaining blocks

14 For Yvonne's small lap quilt on page 35 four Bargello blocks are needed. The other three blocks are made in exactly the same way as the first. Follow steps 1–13 each time to make each of the blocks. The first block can be used as a pattern to check the others against as they progress.

!

Don't attempt to make the other three Bargello blocks simultaneously. It is easy enough to get the pieced strips out of sequence making a single block without adding to the pitfalls with multi-cutting and stitching. Just work through one block at a time.

MATCHING AND JOINING THE BLOCKS

1 There is a lot of flexibility in each completed Bargello block. Use the steam iron to press each block as described in step 13, keeping the first block as the model and trying to press the other blocks to match the dimensions of the original. Press the vertical seams of block 2 in the same direction as those of block 1 – these will become the top row of blocks in the quilt. Press the vertical seams of blocks 3 and 4 (the bottom row of blocks) in the *opposite* direction to blocks 1 and 2. If the top and bottom edges of the first block have been trimmed, follow the trimming on the other three so that all four blocks are as near identical as possible.

2 To make the design flow across the quilt an extra pieced strip is needed between the top two blocks, and a second strip between the bottom two blocks (Fig 11).

Fig 11

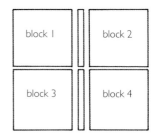

To make these, from the leftover fabric tube, cut two bands each 1in (2.5cm) wide. On each band undo the seam between fabric 1 and fabric 8. Place one pieced strip between the two top blocks with fabric 1 at the top and fabric 8 at the bottom (Fig 12).

Fig 12

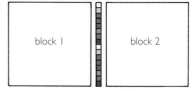

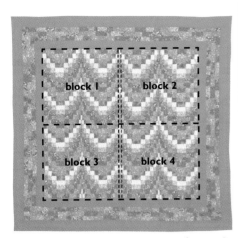

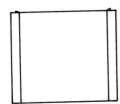

This shows how the two extra pieced strips fit between blocks 1 and 2, and blocks 3 and 4.

3 Pin and stitch the strip to the blocks, matching seams carefully. Press the seams from the front of the work in the same direction as the other seams in the blocks.

4 In the same way pin and stitch the other pieced strip to the bottom blocks. Press the seams in the same direction as the other seams in these blocks.

5 Pin and stitch the top half of the design to the bottom half, matching seams carefully. The seams should be lying in opposite directions so will lock together. Press this long seam to one side, ironing from the front of the work.

ADDING THE BORDERS

1 Inner border: Measure the quilt from top to bottom down its centre. Cut two strips of the chosen inner border fabric measuring 2½in (6.4cm) wide and a length to match the centre measurement. Pin and stitch these two strips to either side of the quilt (Fig 13). Press the seams outwards, away from the quilt.

Fig 13

2 Measure the quilt from side to side across the centre. Cut two strips of the border fabric 2½in (6.4cm) wide and a length to match the quilt measurement. Pin and stitch the two long strips to the top and bottom of the quilt (Fig 14). Press seams outwards, away from the quilt.

Fig 14

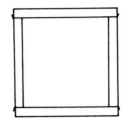

3 Middle border: From leftover strips from the Bargello (1½in/3.8cm wide) cut off pieces 3in (7.6cm) long. Join these together in a length to match the sides of the quilt. Make six of these lengths and stitch them together into two bands each of three lengths, staggering seams as in Fig 15. Press the bands from the front of the work.

Fig 15

4 Pin and stitch a pieced band to either side of the quilt. Press the seams outwards, away from the quilt (Fig 16).

Fig 16

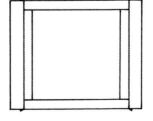

5 Make two similar bands in a length to match the top and bottom of the quilt. Pin and stitch these to the quilt (Fig 17).

Fig 17

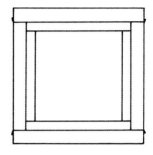

6 Outer border: Add this final border from the same fabric as you used for the inner border, also cut 2½in (6.4cm) wide.

QUILTING

Yvonne quilted her design by machine, stitching diagonally across all the pieces of fabric 1 and of fabric 5 to accentuate the rise and fall of the design. She machine-quilted large triangles across all three borders. The quilt was bound in the same fabric as the inner and outer borders (see Binding a Quilt, page 133).

Buzz-Saw

This chapter features two quilts that use Buzz-Saw blocks but in different layouts. Mavis Hall's Smart and Snazzy red and blue quilt (opposite) has a very regular arrangement. The Buzz-Saw block looks similar to Log Cabin with the added bonus of the saw-tooth seams that run diagonally across it (see Fig 1 below). Strips of different fabrics are combined to make each block, giving it a real scrap look and using up some of those stashed fabrics. The almost circular buzz-saw effect is created by joining four blocks together (see Fig 2). Heather Thomas' Shades of Autumn quilt on page 45 has a softer look, using autumnal colours. She has allowed four blocks to break into the wide border, giving the quilt an attractive irregularity.

Smart and Snazzy

Finished block size 7½in x 7½in (19cm x 19cm)
Finished size of Buzz-Saw square
(four blocks joined) 15in x 15in (38cm x 38cm)
Finished quilt size 72in x 87in (183cm x 221cm)

THE QUILT STORY

Mavis Hall at last found the ideal design in the Buzz-Saw to use two collections of red and blue fabrics that she had bought specifically and was patiently hoarding until inspiration struck. She used one background fabric throughout, although you could use up some of your fabric stash by having a mixture of similar fabrics.

FABRIC REQUIREMENTS

If you wish to make a different size quilt, see page 47.

◆ For the Smart and Snazzy quilt you will need two different sets of fabrics (A and B) that will blend together to make the Buzz-Saw design, plus one set of fabrics for the background. Find as many as you can for a scrap look. Each block starts with an 8½in x 8½in (21.6cm x 21.6cm) cut square of fabric.

◆ Buzz-Saw blocks: twenty squares in each set of fabrics, plus forty strips of assorted fabrics from each set, each cut 2in x 8in (5cm x 20.3cm). A total of about 1½yd (1.37m) in each of the two fabric groups is needed.

◆ Background fabric: 2½yd (2.3m), either all one fabric or a collection used together for a more scrappy look, plus forty squares each 8½in x 8½in used in the design.

◆ Borders and binding: 1yd (1m) of background fabric for the first border and 1yd (1m) of an extra fabric to set off the design for the final border and binding.

◆ Wadding and backing fabric: at least 2in (5cm) larger than finished quilt size.

Fig 1

Fig 2

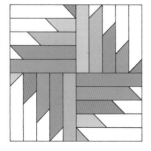

The spiky-angled seams on the Buzz-Saw design are created by stitching diagonally across larger squares of fabric, then cutting into strips and rearranging.

STITCH-A-STRIP

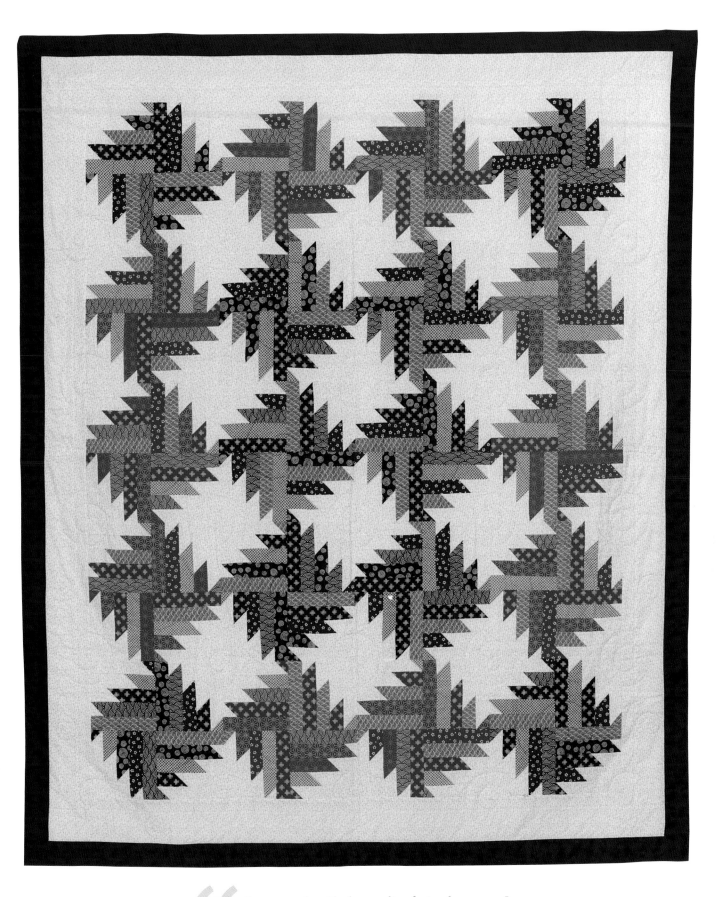

Buzz-Saw seemed an ideal masculine design for my son. I tried to create movement with circular quilting both in the saws and the background. I thought the dark blue and red fabrics in my stash were very appropriate. (Mavis Hall)

Construction

MAKING SET A BLOCKS

1 From the fabrics chosen for the first set of blocks (A) cut twenty squares each measuring 8½in x 8½in (21.6cm x 21.6cm), varying the fabrics as much as possible. From these fabrics also cut forty strips, as varied as possible, each measuring 2in x 8in (5cm x 20.3cm). From the background fabric or group of fabrics just cut twenty squares each 8½in x 8½in (21.6cm x 21.6cm). Do *not* cut extra strips from the background fabrics.

2 Place a cut square of background fabric on to a square of buzz-saw fabric chosen from set A with right sides facing, matching edges carefully. Pin the layers together. Draw a diagonal line across the background square (Fig 3).

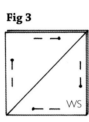

Fig 3

To machine a line on either side of a drawn line at exactly ¼in (6mm) try the following:

a) use a special ¼in (6mm) foot on the machine;

b) if your machine has the facility, move the needle until the distance between it and the side of your usual machine foot is exactly ¼in (6mm);

c) draw in a stitching line ¼in (6mm) away from the diagonal line on both sides, using a different colour marking pencil to avoid confusion.

---

3 Machine a line of stitching on either side of the drawn line at a distance of exactly ¼in (6mm) (Fig 4).

Fig 4

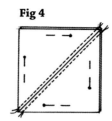

4 Cut along the drawn diagonal line. Press each half open to make a square, ironing the seam towards the buzz-saw fabric (Fig 5). You will now have two squares made from these fabrics.

Fig 5

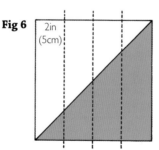

RS

WS

5 Trim the pieced squares to exactly 8in x 8in (20.3cm x 20.3cm) – use a square ruler and match the diagonal line on the ruler with the diagonal seam on the fabric square as you trim.

6 Cut each trimmed square vertically into four strips, each 2in (5cm) wide (Fig 6).

Fig 6

2in (5cm)

7 Repeat this with all forty squares cut from the set A fabrics, each square matched with a similar cut square of background fabric.

Sorting the strips

8 Make four separate piles of strips as in Fig 7. Each pile should contain forty strips, each strip having the same arrangement of pieces but using a variety of buzz-saw fabrics from set A together with the background fabric.

Fig 7

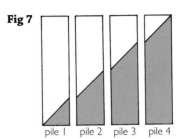

pile 1   pile 2   pile 3   pile 4

9 Make a fifth pile of the forty complete strips cut from the assorted buzz-saw fabrics.

10 Take one strip from each pile, making sure that all the buzz-saw fabrics are different and arrange them as in Fig 8.

Fig 8

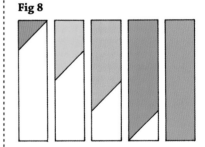

11 Pin and stitch the strips together using a ¼in (6mm) seam. Take care to match the top and bottom of the strips so that the edges of the completed block are level, not uneven. Press the seams to one side, ironing from the front of the work.

> **!** The block should measure 8in x 8in (20.3cm x 20.3cm). It will probably be fine from top to bottom of the strips but must also be 8in (20.3cm) across the strips. If it isn't, check your ¼in (6mm) seam allowance and adjust if necessary.

12 Pin and stitch the rest of the blocks in set A fabrics in the same way. Press the seams to one side as before.

Time and thread can be saved by stitching the first pair of strips in every block one after the other (see Fig 9 below). Cut the threads to separate the stitched pairs of strips. Pin and stitch the third strip to each block one after the other in the same way. Cut the threads between each block. Add the fourth strip and finally the fifth strip to each block in a chain, as before.

Fig 9

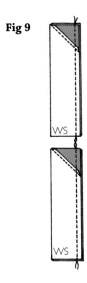

MAKING SET B BLOCKS

Using the second set of buzz-saw fabrics, follow steps 1–12 to make forty blocks.

Joining the blocks into squares

13 Take four blocks made from set A of the buzz-saw fabrics and arrange them into the buzz-saw design shown in Fig 2 on page 40. To create a good balance, choose blocks where the different fabrics are distributed evenly over the design.

14 Pin and stitch the top two blocks together. Press the seam to one side (Fig 10), ironing from the front of the work.

Fig 10

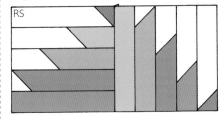

15 Pin and stitch the bottom two blocks together (Fig 11). Press the seam in the *opposite* direction to that of the top row, ironing from the front of the work.

Fig 11

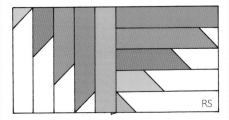

16 Pin and stitch the top pair of blocks to the bottom pair, matching the centre seams carefully. Press the long seam to one side.

If the seams are very bulky it might be better to press this long seam open to distribute the bulk more evenly. Either way is allowed – it just depends on how thick the fabrics are and what you feel looks best.

17 In the same way, arrange all the remaining blocks made from set A of fabrics into fours in the design shown in Fig 2 and stitch them together. There should be ten large squares altogether using set A fabrics.

18 Repeat this to make ten large squares from the blocks using the set B fabrics.

JOINING THE BLOCKS

1 Arrange the twenty squares as in Mavis' Smart and Snazzy quilt on page 41, or in another arrangement that pleases you. There should be five vertical rows of buzz-saw squares with four buzz-saw squares in each horizontal row.

2 Pin and stitch the top row of squares together. Press the seams to one side, ironing from the front of the work.

3 Pin and stitch the second row of squares together. Press the seams in the *opposite* direction to row 1, ironing from the front of the work. Continue to pin and stitch each row, pressing seams in alternate directions to help lock them.

4 Join the rows together, matching seams carefully. Press seams to one side from the front.

ADDING THE BORDERS

Mavis' quilt was edged with a border of background fabric to allow the Buzz-Saw blocks to 'float'. This border strip was cut 4½in (11.4cm) wide, finishing 4in (10cm) wide. The second border of navy fabric was cut 2½in (6.3cm) wide, finishing 2in (5cm) wide. The same fabric was used to bind the quilt (see Bordering a Quilt page 128).

QUILTING

Mavis hand quilted around each Buzz-Saw block and then quilted spirals in the centre of each one. She quilted similar spirals in the large areas of background between each block and smaller spirals in the background around the edges of the design.

Shades of Autumn

THE QUILT STORY

This second quilt, made by Heather Thomas, uses the Buzz-Saw block in a very different arrangement. For this design Heather used all leftovers from the sampler quilt she made from *Lynne Edwards' New Sampler Quilt Book* (D&C, 2000), grouping all the greens together for the set A blocks and the browns for set B blocks. The background is a mix of warm neutrals, again, mainly from her sampler quilt. The block is exactly the same as Smart and Snazzy on page 40, but fewer blocks are needed and the arrangement is completely different. This quilt needs fifty-six blocks in total (twenty-eight blocks in each set of fabrics), creating twelve large squares, plus four half-squares. To make a quilt in a different size, see the advice on page 47.

Finished block size 7½in x 7½in (19cm x 19cm)
Finished size of Buzz-Saw square
(four blocks joined – Fig 12) 15in x 15in (38cm x 38cm)
Finished quilt size 73in x 88in (191cm x 229cm)

FABRIC REQUIREMENTS

For the Shades of Autumn quilt you will need two sets of fabrics (A and B) that blend together for the Buzz-Saw blocks, plus a selection of neutrals for the background. Each block starts with an 8½in x 8½in (21.6cm x 21.6cm) cut square of fabric.

◆ Buzz-Saw blocks: fourteen squares in each set of fabrics are used for this design plus twenty-eight strips of assorted fabrics from each set, each cut 2in x 8in (5cm x 20.3cm). A total of about 1¼yd (1.15m) in each of the two fabric groups is needed.

◆ Assorted background fabrics: 1¾yd (1.6m).

◆ Borders and binding: an additional 1½yd (1.4m) of one of the background fabrics is needed for the wide border on which the buzz-saw design 'floats'; 1yd (1m) of brown fabric for the narrow second border plus binding; 1yd (1m) of green fabric for the wide outer border.

◆ Wadding and backing fabric: at least 2in (5cm) larger than finished quilt size.

Construction

Follow the method described in steps 2–12 for the Smart and Snazzy quilt (pages 42–43) to make twenty-eight blocks in each set of fabrics, and then continue as follows.

JOINING THE BLOCKS INTO SQUARES

1 Take two blocks made from set A of the buzz-saw fabrics and two blocks made from set B. Arrange them as in Fig 12, with the background fabric all in the centre.

Fig 12

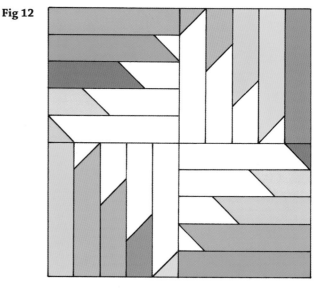

Begun as a present for my son, this is essentially a scrap quilt. The fabrics in the collection are leftovers from trips to America, including Lancaster County. The choice of colours reflects my love of natural, muted shades, which have led to a more co-ordinated result than I imagined. My quilt is hand quilted and perhaps could have more quilting in the border – the difficulty is knowing when to stop. (Heather Thomas)

2 Pin and stitch the top two blocks together. Press the seam to one side, ironing from the front (Fig 13).

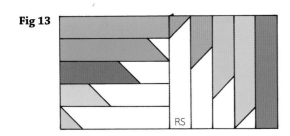

Fig 13

3 Pin and stitch the bottom two blocks together. Press the seams in the *opposite* direction to that of the top row, ironing from the front (Fig 14).

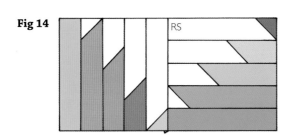

Fig 14

4 Pin and stitch the top pair of blocks to the bottom pair, matching the centre seams carefully. Press the long seam to one side or open if preferred to distribute the fabric bulk more evenly.

5 In the same way arrange forty-four of the remaining blocks into fours, as in the design in Fig 12. There should be twelve large squares altogether with eight blocks left over for the border.

6 Arrange the twelve squares into four rows each of three squares and stitch them together, one row at a time (Fig 15).

Fig 15

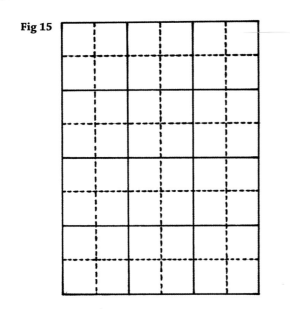

Making the background border

7 From the background fabric cut the following: eight squares each 8in x 8in (20.3cm x 20.3cm); two strips each 8in x 23in (20.3cm x 58.4cm); two strips each 8in x 38in (20.3cm x 96.5cm).

8 Take two Buzz-Saw blocks, one made from set A fabrics and one from set B. Arrange these together with one 38in (96.5cm) long strip and one square of background fabric (Fig 16). Pin and stitch these together to make one long length for a side border. Repeat this to make another length for the other side border. Press seams to one side from the front.

Fig 16

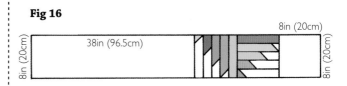

9 Pin and stitch these to the sides of the quilt, matching seams carefully (Fig 17). Press seams outwards, away from the quilt.

Fig 17

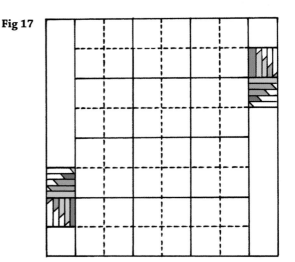

10 Arrange the remaining long strips and squares of background fabric with the last four Buzz-Saw blocks into two lengths, each as in Fig 18. These will make the top and bottom border strips. Pin and stitch these to the top and bottom of the quilt, matching seams carefully (Fig 19).

Fig 18

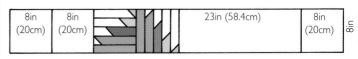

STITCH-A-STRIP

Fig 19

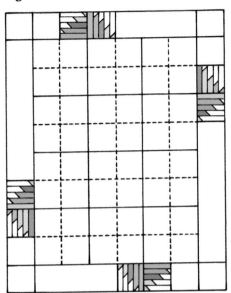

ADDING THE EXTRA BORDERS

Heather first added a narrow border of background fabric to allow the extra Buzz-Saw blocks to float. This border strip was cut 2in (5cm) wide, finishing 1½in (3.8cm) wide. The narrow brown border was cut 1½in (3.8cm) wide finishing 1in (2.5cm) wide. The final wide green border was cut 4½in (11.4cm) wide, finishing 4in wide (see Bordering a Quilt page 128). The quilt was bound in the same brown fabric as was used for the narrow inner border (see Binding a Quilt page 133).

QUILTING

Heather hand quilted three squares on point within each other in each of the Buzz-Saw blocks and repeated these in the large areas of background fabric between each buzz-saw. The same design continues in the wide border where it appears as a series of triangles.

MAKING A DIFFERENT SIZED QUILT

To make a quilt in a different size from Mavis and Heather, you will need to calculate how many of the large buzz-saw squares (Fig 2, page 40) are needed for your quilt. Each square measures 15in x 15in (38cm x 38cm).

Cut the *same* number of 8½in (21.6cm) squares from each of the two sets of buzz-saw fabrics and twice that number of 2in x 8in (5cm x 20.3cm) strips.

Cut *twice* the number of 8½in (21.6cm) squares from the background fabrics, e.g., if twelve large buzz-saw squares are needed for your quilt, cut twelve squares measuring 8½in x 8½in (21.6cm x 21.6cm) and twenty-four strips from each of the two sets of buzz-saw fabrics.

Cut twenty-four squares measuring 8½in x 8½in (21.6cm x 21.6cm) from the background fabrics.

Squaring It Up

Mail-order quilt companies feed our lust for handling piles of fabric by sending samples of their current stock. The true quilt addict can sign up and pay to receive monthly packages of tasty 5in (12.7cm) squares or even larger pieces, all waiting to be thumbed through and drooled over. Do we do anything with these goodies? Not often. We just watch them piling up and enjoy the view. Well, here is a group of quilts that will have you using up some of these piles – and the more fabrics to be used up, the better. Start with Squares on Point, overleaf, or the contemporary effect of boxed squares on page 58.

Squares on Point

I have always loved designs that use squares or blocks arranged on point, that is, turned through 45 degrees so that the corners point north, south, west and east. Using up your stash of fabric squares to make this striking quilt (right) will mean some tedious cutting up of small pieces into even smaller squares or strips, but if this is spread over several sessions it can be soothingly mindless. And the results are so attractive that it's well worth it, plus you'll have that virtuous glow that comes from using up at least some of the collected goodies, at last. Using the same technique, Pauline Bugg used squares on point to create her delicately coloured Pastel Pastiche quilt on page 57.

Crystal Squares

Square size 2½in x 2½in (6.3cm x 6.3cm)
Finished quilt size 65in x 65in (165cm x 165cm)

THE QUILT STORY

When I saw Pauline's quilt I went to my own stash, inspired to make something similar. It didn't take long to realize that despite the groaning shelves of fabric I just didn't have enough different pieces in suitable colours to make a decent-sized quilt. So I decided to make a specific design of squares rather like a cross stitch design, using several completely different groups of colours. I chose to cut 2½in x 2½in (6.3cm x 6.3cm) squares because I had a large collection of samples that were 5in (12.7cm) square so this size used the fabric most economically.

FABRIC REQUIREMENTS

◆ Five colour teams of fabric are used in this quilt with as many different fabrics as possible within each team (see advice, left). Fig 1 (overleaf) shows the positioning of each colour in the quilt, labelled A to E:

Team A (pink/cerise shades) – 97 squares each cut 2½in x 2½in (6.3cm x 6.3cm);

Team B (purple shades) – 348 squares each cut 2½in x 2½in (6.3cm x 6.3cm);

Team C (pale pastel shades) – 232 squares each cut 2½in x 2½in (6.3cm x 6.3cm);

Team D (lavender shades) – 112 squares each cut 2½in x 2½in (6.3cm x 6.3cm);

Team E (turquoise/teal shades) – 136 squares each cut 2½in x 2½in (6.3cm x 6.3cm).

◆ Border: ½yd (0.5m) of fabric, for a border with a finished width of 2½in (6.3cm).

◆ Binding: ½yd (0.5m) of fabric.

◆ Wadding and backing fabric: at least 2in (5cm) larger than finished quilt size.

Sorting the fabrics

Ideally, at least twenty different fabrics should make up each colour team. Sort out possible fabrics into piles and include less obvious candidates as well as the co-ordinating members of the team. Needing so many fabrics means that anything vaguely resembling the team colour has to be included, which is good as it is these oddballs that create interest in a scrap quilt. Team B and C use far more squares than the other three teams, so look out for more fabrics to include in these shades.

The design is made in four identical quarters following a chart (Fig 1 overleaf) for stitching the fabric squares into rows. The four sections are then joined to complete the design.

Construction

CUTTING THE SQUARES

1 Deal with the fabrics from one team at a time. Count how many fabrics there are and how many squares are needed for the design (see Fig 1). From this you can work out roughly how many squares should be cut from each fabric. Keep a small box or tray for each colour and place the squares of fabric in it as they are cut. Don't plan to cut all the squares for the quilt at once – you'll die of boredom or collapse with Rotary Cutter Fatigue – do this preparation in between other tasks over a few days. The reward will be when the stitching begins and the quilt grows row by speedy row.

> When stitching together a series of fabrics in a wide range of colours, it's impractical to keep changing thread colour, so use a medium-tone dull grey throughout, as this is the least conspicuous on a wide range of fabrics.

Fig 1

Stitching section one

Rather than joining the squares together in long rows diagonally across the entire quilt, it is constructed in four sections each making one quarter of the quilt, plus one extra square. This square forms the centre of the quilt when the completed quarters are finally joined to it (Fig 2). Each quarter section is made by stitching squares into rows. The four sections are identical in layout and colour placement, although the individual squares of fabric will vary because they are picked out at random.

Each quarter of the design is constructed from twenty-one rows of joined squares (Fig 3). The first row is the longest, with twenty-one squares stitched together. Row 2 has one square less, row 3 one less again and so on until the last triumphant row 21, which is just one square.

Fig 2

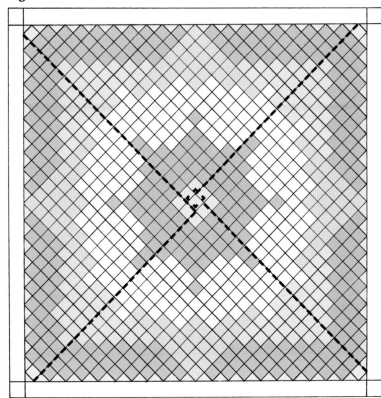

Fig 3

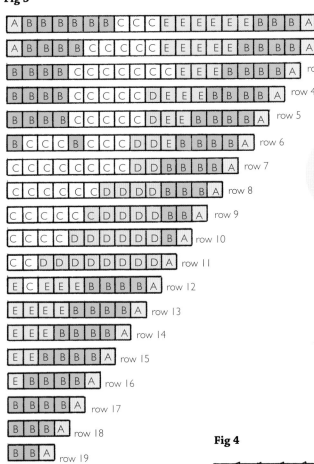

Don't spend time agonizing over which fabric square looks good joined to its neighbour: you just need to avoid placing two squares of the same fabric together, but no other considerations are necessary. Just take a square of fabric from the appropriate team and stitch it on.

2 1st row: Follow the chart in Fig 3 for the sequence of fabrics to be used in row 1. Pin and stitch the twenty-one squares together using a smaller stitch than for dressmaking and the usual ¼in (6mm) seam (Fig 4). Press the seams all to one side, ironing from the front of the work.

Fig 4

3 2nd row: Follow the chart in Fig 3 for the sequence of fabric squares for row 2. Pin and stitch the twenty squares together as before (Fig 5). Press the seams in the opposite direction to row 1, ironing from the front of the work. This will help the seams to lock together when the rows are joined.

Fig 5

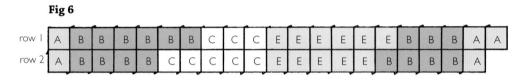

4 Place rows 1 and 2 together as in Fig 6, checking that no squares of the same fabric are lying next to each other. Now is the time to correct this if necessary. Pin and stitch the two rows together, matching seams carefully. Press the long seam towards row 2, ironing from the front of the work.

Fig 6

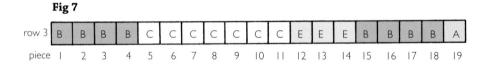

5 3rd row: Follow the chart in Fig 4 for row 3. Pin and stitch the nineteen squares together (Fig 7). Press the seams to one side in the same direction as row 1.

Fig 7

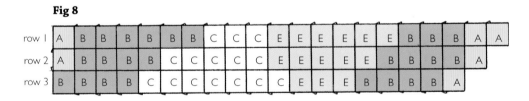

6 Place the joined rows 1 and 2 together with row 3 in the arrangement shown in Fig 8. Check that no squares of the same fabric are lying next to each other in row 2 and row 3 before pinning and stitching row 3 on to row 2, matching seams carefully. Press the long seam back towards row 2, ironing from the front.

Fig 8

7 In the same way follow the chart in Fig 3 to make row 4 (eighteen squares). Press the seams in the same direction as those of row 2. Pin and stitch it to row 3 (Fig 9). Press the long seam towards row 4.

Fig 9

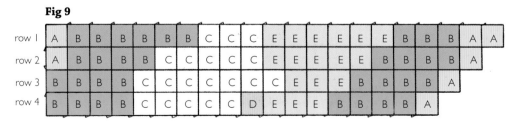

8 Continue to make each row as in Fig 3, pressing the seams of each row in alternate directions before pinning and stitching it to the previous row, as before. The long seams also get pressed in alternate directions as each row is joined. Every row gets one square shorter, so the task gets quicker as you go along.

9 When section 1 is complete check it against the diagram in Fig 3 to make sure that the colour teams are all in the right position.

10 Sections 2, 3 and 4 are made in exactly the same way as section 1. Follow steps 2–8 each time to make each of the three remaining sections. Now that one section has been made it can be used as a pattern to check the others against as they progress.

If you are an ace machinist, save time and thread by making the other three sections of the quilt simultaneously. Instead of making row 1 followed by row 2, make three versions of row 1 at the same time, chaining the squares together as in Fig 10. Cut the threads between each row after the three versions of row 1 are completed. Press seams to one side, all in the same direction. Make three versions of row 2 in the same way. Join each pair of row 1 to row 2 together before making three versions of row 3, and so on.

JOINING THE SECTIONS

1 One extra square of fabric A is used as the centre of the quilt. Lay section 1 on a flat surface with right side *upwards*. Place the extra square of fabric A on to the corner square of section 1 with right side *down* and edges matching (Fig 11).

Fig 11

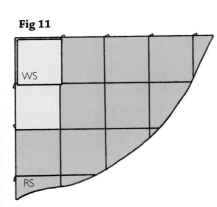

2 Pin and stitch part-way along the pinned seam, leaving the bottom 1in (2.5cm) *unstitched* (Fig 12).

Fig 12

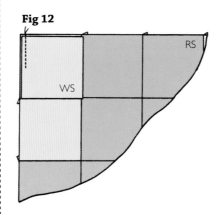

3 Open the square out, away from the pieced section, pressing the seam allowance towards the square (Fig 13).

Fig 13

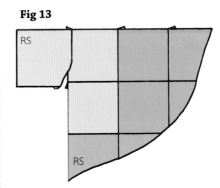

4 Pin and stitch section 2 to the centre square and section 1, matching seams carefully (Fig 14). Press the long seam towards section 1.

Fig 14

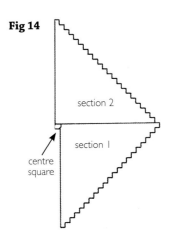

section 2

section 1

centre square

Fig 10

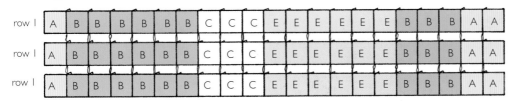

row 1	A	B	B	B	B	B	B	C	C	C	E	E	E	E	E	E	B	B	B	A	A
row 1	A	B	B	B	B	B	B	C	C	C	E	E	E	E	E	E	B	B	B	A	A
row 1	A	B	B	B	B	B	B	C	C	C	E	E	E	E	E	E	B	B	B	A	A

5 Pin and stitch section 3 to the centre square and section 2, matching seams carefully (Fig 15).

Fig 15

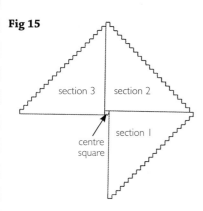

section 3   section 2

centre square

section 1

6 Pin and stitch section 4 to the centre square and section 3 as before. Press the long seam towards section 3.

7 Finally, pin and stitch the last seam of the design, joining section 4 to section 1, continuing the stitches of the original part-stitched seam. Press the seam towards section 4.

Trimming the edges

8 The squares on the outer edges of the quilt need to be trimmed down so that the border strip can be added. Lay one edge of the quilt horizontally on a cutting mat and place a rotary cutter on it. Line up the points of the last row of finished squares with the ¼in (6mm) marking on the ruler, as shown in Fig 16.

Fig 16

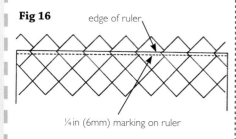

edge of ruler

¼in (6mm) marking on ruler

Cut along the edge of the ruler to trim the quilt to a straight edge ¼in (6mm) beyond the points of the finished squares (Fig 17). Repeat this around all the edges of the quilt.

Fig 17

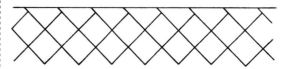

ADDING THE BORDER

1 Measure across the quilt, not along its edge as here all the squares have been cut across the grain or weave of the fabric and are very stretchy. Measure in several places and both down and across the quilt. In an ideal world all the measurements will be the same but this is hardly realistic. Take an average measurement of those you have made and use this for the length of the border strips.

2 Cut four strips of the fabric chosen for the border, each 3in (7.6cm) wide and in a length to match the measurement taken from the quilt. Cut four squares for the cornerstones, each 3in x 3in (7.6cm x 7.6cm).

3 Place the quilt on a flat surface and pin and stitch a strip of border fabric to each side, easing the quilt edge to fit the border strip if necessary (Fig 18). Press seams out, away from the quilt.

4 Stitch a 3in (7.6cm) cornerstone square to either end of the remaining two strips of border fabric (Fig 19). Press the seams towards the long strip.

Fig 18

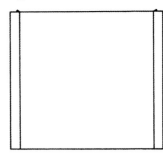

Fig 19

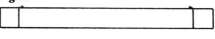

5 Pin and stitch these border strips to the top and bottom of the quilt, matching seams carefully and easing in any fullness in the quilt edge (Fig 20). Press the seams outwards, away from the quilt.

Fig 20

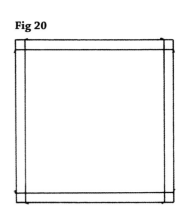

QUILTING

This quilt was just one too many for me to be inspired to quilt. I handed it over to Jenny Spencer from Mildenhall in Suffolk who uses a long-arm quilting machine. Jenny used curving lines of quilting, which not only softened the design but also contrasted well with the linear aspects of the quilt. I was really pleased with the finished design and enjoyed seeing someone else's ideas used on my quilt.

Pastel Pastiche

When Pauline Bugg first started patchwork she sent for all the sample squares of fabric from the mail-order quilt shops and avidly collected fat quarters of the wonderful fabrics on offer in shops and at quilt shows without any specific projects in mind. Some years later she decided she needed to clear her shelves a little by making scrap quilts, preferably from squares so that the small samples could be used up as well as the larger pieces, and this lovely quilt justifies her collecting habit.

> *This quilt is made from the leftovers from another quilt plus a few more 'must-have' fabrics. The combination of small on point squares, soft pastel colours and wavy quilted lines have resulted in this simple but pretty quilt, which has become one of my favourites. (Pauline Bugg)*

Boxed Squares

There is no formal design to this easy but highly versatile quilt – just keep making the blocks using as many fabrics as you can find that look good together in the quilt. You could make great inroads into your fabric stash and achieve a truly scrap-quilt effect by making every block with a different fabric, or control the colour scheme more by limiting the fabrics, to twelve or fourteen, as Pauline Bugg did for her Boxing Clever quilt (opposite). The border and binding of your quilt can also be made up of different fabrics: the binding around the edge of this quilt ties in with the colours used within the quilt and allowed Pauline to use up quite small fabric pieces.

Boxing Clever

Finished block size 6in x 6in (15cm x 15cm)
Finished quilt size 71in x 89in (180.3cm x 226cm)

THE QUILT STORY

The boxed square design (Fig 1) is a classic quilt pattern which I first saw in an Amish cot quilt that is part of Sara Miller's fine collection of beautiful Amish crib quilts. I love the rich, plain colours so typical of Amish quilts, as does Heather Jackson who made her own version in softer shades (see page 62). As a real contrast the single-bed project quilt by Pauline Bugg (shown right) is made from 154 blocks – 11 blocks across and 14 down – using the latest range of zingy fabrics she saw while working in a quilt shop in Suffolk, England. She used fourteen different fabrics in her quilt, starting with half a yard of each, so of course had some left over. . .

Fig 1

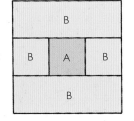

FABRIC REQUIREMENTS

◆ For a single-bed quilt, you can use as many different fabrics as you can find, making sure that you have a total of at least 6 yards or metres of 42in (106.7cm) wide fabrics.

◆ For a queen-size quilt like Heather's (page 62), 9 yards or metres are needed for a total of 169 blocks (13 rows of blocks, each row containing 13 blocks).

◆ Border and binding: an extra ½ yard or metre is needed for the quilt border. The narrow binding is made from joined pieces of all the fabrics used in the blocks.

◆ Wadding and backing fabric: at least 2in (5cm) larger than finished quilt size.

> *What a great design this is to make! The speed with which the blocks come together is exciting and then there is all the fun of arranging them to make a design that balances all those different fabrics. (Pauline Bugg)*

 Each pair of blocks takes just one strip each of two fabrics cut into five pieces. The block is simple and quick to piece with no seams that need matching, yet it is stunningly effective.

SQUARING IT UP

Construction

1 Choose two fabrics that look good together (shown as A and B in Figs 3a and 3b). From each fabric cut one strip measuring 2½in x 21in (6.3cm x 53.3cm). Cut the strip into pieces as shown in Fig 2: three squares each 2½in x 2½in (6.3cm x 6.3cm) and two strips each 2½in x 6½in (6.3cm x 16.5cm).

Fig 2

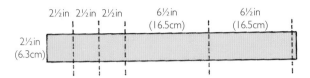

2 Your fabrics pieces are now combined to make two blocks as in Figs 3a and 3b.

Fig 3a

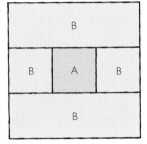

Fig 3b

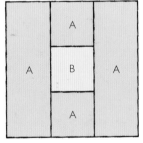

To do this, take one square 2½in x 2½in (6.3cm x 6.3cm) from the cut strip of fabric A and two similar squares from the strip of fabric B. Pin and stitch them together as in Fig 4, using a ¼in (6mm) seam and slightly smaller stitch than for dressmaking. Press the seams towards fabric B, ironing from the front of the work.

Fig 4

3 Pin and stitch one of the 6½in (16.5cm) long strips cut from fabric B to the top of the block (Fig 5). Press the seam towards the long strip of fabric B. Always iron from the front of the work.

Fig 5

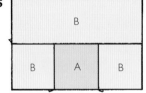

4 Pin and stitch the remaining 6½in (16.5cm) strip of fabric B to the bottom of the block (Fig 6). Press the seam towards the long strip of fabric B.

Fig 6

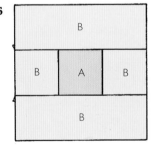

The 6½in (16.5cm) long strip should match the joined squares exactly. If not, now is the time to check your ¼in (6mm) seam allowance and adjust it so that both sections are the same length.

5 Now repeat the process to make a second block using the remaining cut square of fabric B as the centre of the block and the surrounding pieces from the two squares and two strips of fabric A (Fig 7).

Fig 7

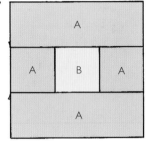

6 Choose two more fabrics that will look good combined in the block. From each fabric cut a strip measuring 2½in x 21in (6.3cm x 53.3cm) as before. Follow steps 1–5 to make two blocks in these new fabrics.

Each block should measure 6½in x 6½in (16.5cm x 16.5cm) at this stage. Measure the blocks as you make them and, if necessary, trim them to the correct size. If they are coming up smaller than they should, just trim all the blocks to this smaller measurement so they will fit together easily when joined – all this means is a slightly smaller quilt.

7 Now there'll be no stopping you: just keep taking two strips of fabric that you want to combine and make two blocks with them. Add more fabrics or use different combinations of a limited number of fabrics as you wish.

ARRANGING THE BLOCKS

This is the most important element of this design. If possible pin the blocks on to a wall or design board so that you can balance the colours of the blocks effectively. If this is not possible lay them on the floor and stand on a chair or steps to view the overall design from as far away as possible. The blocks are turned alternately through 180 degrees when joined together to make a more interesting design with the seams. This also means fewer seams to match when joining the blocks, which is a bonus (Fig 8).

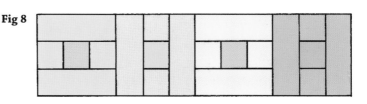

When arranging the blocks, to see which of them stand out as more dominant than the others, half-close your eyes as you view the design. The strong tones will leap out at you and it is these that you need to spread around the quilt to help the visual balance.

ASSEMBLING THE QUILT

1 Once the positioning is done, number the blocks of the top row before taking them to the sewing machine to stitch them together. Pin and stitch the top row of blocks together with the usual ¼in (6mm) seam. Press the seams all to one side, ironing from the front of the work.

2 Number the blocks of row two before piling them up and bringing them to the machine. Pin and stitch the second row of blocks together as before. Press the seams in the *opposite* direction to those of row one. This

means that when the long rows are joined the seams will lock together.

3 Continue to pin and stitch each row of blocks, pressing seams in alternate directions to help lock them.

4 Join the rows together, matching seams carefully. Press seams to one side from the front of the work.

ADDING THE BORDER

Pauline's quilt was framed with a strip of fabric that is also used in the blocks, cut 2½in (6.3cm) wide and finishing 2in (5cm) wide (see Bordering a Quilt page 128).

QUILTING

Pauline quilted her piece by machining in gentle curves running from top to bottom and side to side on the quilt (Fig 9). The multi-fabric binding is made from left-over strips from the quilt cut into 2½in (6.3cm) lengths and joined together.

SQUARING IT UP

Fig 9

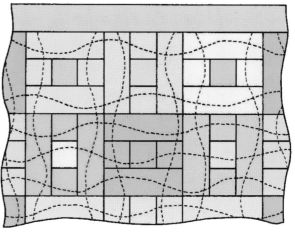

Box-Brownie

Heather Jackson's alternate version of the Boxed Squares quilt has some different blocks scattered throughout the design. In these blocks she replaced the simple centre square with a miniature version of the Boxed Square (see below). The centre unit was introduced specifically to make the left-over bits of fabric go further and really use up the scraps.

After hoarding this fabric for far too long, I decided that the boxed squares design would allow it to be seen at its best. The square-within-a-square centres meant that I wasted absolutely nothing. I kept the quilting as invisible as possible because I loved the simplicity of the pieced top.
(Heather Jackson)

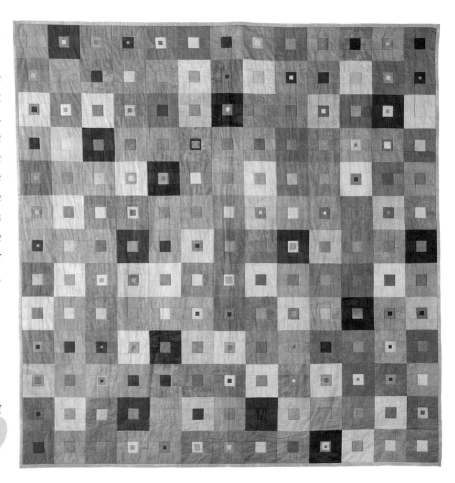

SQUARING IT UP

MAKING A MINIATURE BOXED SQUARE UNIT

Cut one square of fabric for the centre measuring 1¼in x 1¼in (3.2cm x 3.2cm). For the surrounding frame from a different fabric cut two squares 1¼in x 1¼in (3.2cm x 3.2cm) and two strips 1¼in x 2¾in (3.2cm x 7cm). Make up the little block in the same way as the original blocks. The new block should measure 2¾in x 2¾in (7cm x 7cm) at this stage. Trim the block down to 2½in x 2½in (6.3cm x 6.3cm). This miniature unit is now used as the centre square for a block in the original sizing (Fig 10). Make as many versions of this alternative block as you wish and distribute them around the quilt when doing the final arrangement of all the blocks. Fig 11 shows the positioning of the alternative blocks in Heather's Box Brownie quilt.

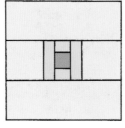
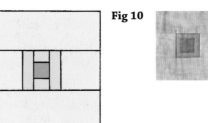

Fig 10

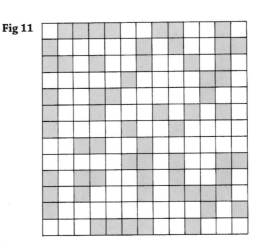

Fig 11

alternative blocks

Over the Rainbow

Collie Parker used one simple block in this vibrant quilt. She used hand-dyed cotton fabrics cut into 2in x 4in (5.1cm x 10.2cm) rectangles throughout to make the design of boxed squares, a variation on the one used in the Boxing Clever quilt on page 59. The centre is made from two rectangles of the same fabric joined to make a square. The outer frame is from six similar rectangles of a contrasting fabric that surrounds the centre.

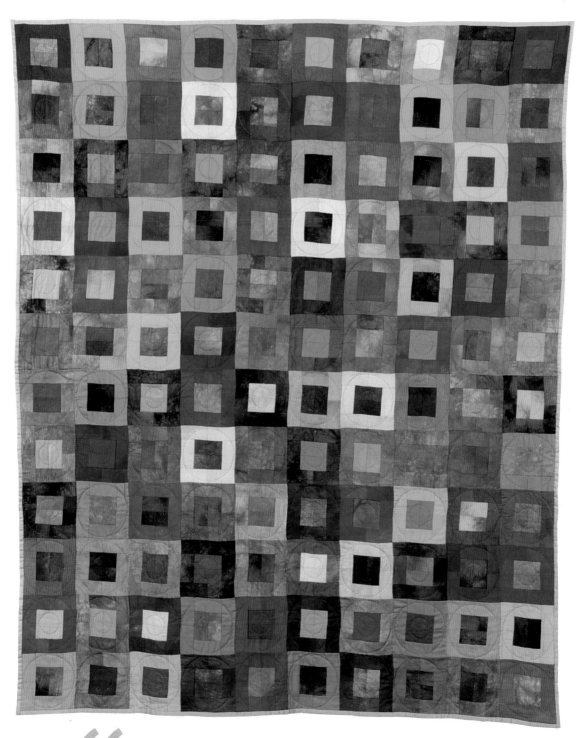

> *This pattern ideally suited my collection of hand dyed and plain cotton sateens and I was very pleased with the result. (Collie Parker)*

Bits and Pieces Quilts

This collection of quilts features the traditional idea of patchwork with differently shaped pieces joined into attractive blocks and designs. All the projects give the opportunity to include many of the fabrics that have been lurking in your stash and make wonderful, often complex, designs. Happily, they all have quick-and-easy methods of construction so they can be achieved without too much effort. Overleaf you will find instructions for two quilts using a tessellated leaf pattern. These are followed on page 74 by two lattice quilt designs, a corner square pattern and, finally on page 90, two stunning star and nine-patch quilts.

Tessellating Leaves

The tessellating leaves pattern is a versatile one, as the two very different quilts in this section show. The block uses a main fabric or collection of fabrics plus a background to create a continuous leaf design, which fits into the next leaf like a jigsaw puzzle, with no spaces in between and is known as a tessellating design (see Fig 1 below). In Sheila Piper's In the Red quilt (right), the block is made in two alternating colour combinations, one with the arrow shape in a main group of fabrics and the other with the arrow shape in a background group of fabrics (Fig 2 below). Alternatively, a true scrap effect with a hint of the abstract can be created by collecting a group of similar fabrics for the leaves and a second group of contrast fabrics for the background leaves, as Shirley Prescott did for her Tumbling Leaves quilt – see instructions on page 71.

In the Red

THE QUILT STORY

Sheila Piper collected a pile of black-and-white-patterned fabrics to make a quilt for her son. She decided to use just one red fabric as the alternating leaf shape, which contrasts wonderfully with the lighter black and white leaves. The small triangles in each block belong to the adjacent leaves, so careful planning is needed to get this effect.

Fig 1

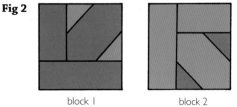

Fig 2

block 1   block 2

Finished block size 6in x 6in (15.2cm x 15.2cm)
Finished quilt size 88in x 64in (223.5cm x 162.6cm)

FABRIC REQUIREMENTS

◆ Seventy-seven blocks are needed for the In the Red quilt – thirty-nine using the black and white fabrics and thirty-eight using the red fabric.

◆ Set 1 leaves: 3yd (2.75m) of assorted fabrics (black and white in Sheila's quilt) plus the second border.

◆ Set 2 leaves: 2½yd (2.3m) of fabric (just one red fabric in Sheila's quilt) plus the third border.

◆ Other borders: 1¼yd (1.15m) of fabric for the 1st and final borders (black in Sheila's quilt).

◆ Wadding and backing fabric: at least 2in (5cm) larger than finished quilt size.

This quilt design used to be made by careful piecing of squares, rectangles and triangles, usually by hand. Now there are quick and easy ways to cut and stitch the design, and the repeated leaf motif means the chance to mix in a lot of different fabrics.

> "I decided I wanted to make my son a quilt while he was away at University. I've always liked red and black quilts and this colour scheme with the added whites seemed to suit the maple leaf design well. *(Sheila Piper)*

Construction

CUTTING THE BLOCKS

1 Each complete leaf can be cut from a rectangle of fabric 9½in x 7in (24.1cm x 17.8cm). Cut thirty-nine rectangles from the first set of fabrics and thirty-eight from the second set.

2 From each rectangle of fabric cut the following:

A – one square 4½in x 4½in (11.4cm x 11.4cm);

B – one rectangle 4½in x 2½in (11.4cm x 6.4cm);

C – one rectangle 6½in x 2½in (16.5cm x 6.4cm);

D – two squares 2½in x 2½in (6.4cm x 6.4cm).

Fig 3 shows the cutting plan for these pieces. Cut out all the pieces for the quilt before you start to assemble them, as you will need a mixture of both sets of fabric for each block.

Fig 3

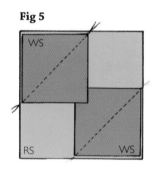

2½in (6.4cm)   2½in (6.4cm)

2½in (6.4cm)   D   D   2½in (6.4cm)

6½ (16.5cm)   C   B   A   4½in (11.4cm)

2½in (6.4cm)   4½in (11.4cm)

The pieces to make each leaf can be cut from a rectangle of fabric measuring 9½in x 7in (24.1cm x 17.8cm), so if an assortment of fabric is being used, a total of thirty-nine rectangles this size will be needed from the first set of fabrics and another thirty-eight from the second set of fabrics.

3 To make block 1: use the same fabric from set 1 throughout the block plus two squares (D) from set 2. Place two smaller squares (D) of set 2 fabric (red) on to the two opposite corners of the large square (A) of set 1 fabric (black and white) with right sides facing, matching edges carefully (Fig 4).

Fig 4

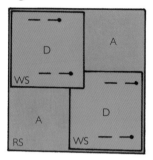

D   A

WS

A   D

RS   WS

4 Stitch across the pinned squares diagonally from corner to corner, as shown in Fig 5.

Fig 5

WS

RS   WS

For a useful tip on adding corners easily, see step 4 of the Scrap Lattice quilt on page 76.

---

5 Trim the excess fabric ¼in (6mm) beyond the stitching line (Fig 6). These trimmed triangles can be used in the border of the quilt as Shirley Prescott did (page 71) or kept for a future miniature quilt. . . possibly. . .

Fig 6

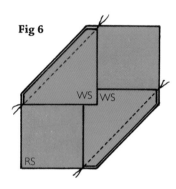

WS   WS

RS

6 Press back the triangles of fabric to make the corners of the square, pressing the seams out towards the corners (Fig 7).

Fig 7

RS

7 Pin and stitch the shorter rectangle (B) of set 1 fabric to the left side of the block (Fig 8). Press the seam outwards from the block, ironing from the front of the work.

Fig 8

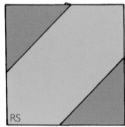

B

RS

8 Pin and stitch the long rectangle (C) of set 1 fabric to the bottom of the block. Press the seam outwards from the block (Fig 9).

Fig 9

Fig 10

9 Make a total of thirty-nine of block 1, using the collection of set 1 fabrics as the leaves. There will be two small squares (D) left over from each 9½in x 7in (24cm x 17.7cm) rectangle of set 1 fabrics, to be used in the other thirty-eight blocks. Do not assemble any of block 2 until you have arranged the first blocks.

ARRANGING AND JOINING THE BLOCKS

1 If you want to make a quilt like Sheila's where each leaf is from a different fabric to its neighbour and using one background fabric throughout, make all thirty-nine of block 1. Arrange them as in Fig 10, leaving spaces for the thirty-eight squares of block 2. You will then be able to see where each small square (D) must be placed to complete each leaf shape in block 2. Pin the small squares in position on the large squares (A) of set 2 fabrics and place them between the completed blocks (Fig 11). Stitch the squares diagonally as described in step 4 and follow steps 5–8 to complete each of the thirty-eight squares of block 2.

Fig 11

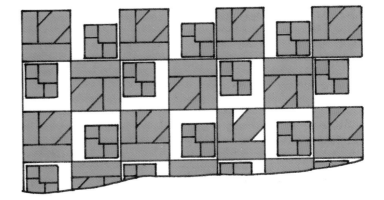

2 Lay out both sets of completed blocks in the alternating arrangement shown in Fig 12.

3 Pin and stitch the top row of seven blocks with the usual ¼in (6mm) seam. Press the seams to one side, ironing from the front of the work.

4 Pin and stitch the second row of seven blocks together. Press the seams in the opposite direction to those of row 1, ironing from the front.

5 Continue to pin and stitch each row, pressing the seams in alternate directions to help lock them.

6 Join the rows together, matching seams carefully. Press seams to one side from the front of the work.

ADDING THE BORDERS

Sheila framed her quilt with a series of simple borders (see Bordering a Quilt page 128).

1st border:
Strips of black fabric cut 2in (5cm) wide and finishing 1½in (3.8cm) wide.

2nd border:
Strips of assorted fabrics from set 1, each cut 4½in x 2½in (11.4cm x 6.4cm). These were joined together to make the pieced border finishing 4in (10cm) wide (Fig 13).

Fig 13

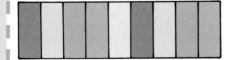

3rd border:
Strips of red fabric cut 2½in (6.4cm) wide, finishing 2in (5cm) wide.

4th border:
strips of black fabric cut 4in (10cm) wide, finishing 3½in (8.9cm) wide.

Fig 12

QUILTING

Sheila quilted the red leaf blocks by hand ½in (1.2cm) inside the edges of the leaf (Fig 14a). She quilted the black and white leaves to represent the veins of the leaves (Fig 14b).

Fig 14a

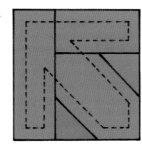

Fig 14b

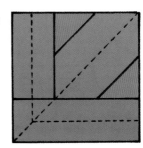

Tumbling Leaves

I found making this quilt using different fabrics for each piece of each leaf a real challenge, as usually my quilts are from a limited number of fabrics rather than from scraps. I was very pleased with the effect of the little pieced border.
(Shirley Prescott)

Finished block size 6in x 6in (15.2cm x 15.2cm)   **Finished quilt size** 51½in x 51½in (130.8cm x 130.8cm)

THE QUILT STORY

For this lap quilt using a tessellating leaves pattern, collecting a group of similar fabrics for the leaves and a second group of contrast fabrics for the background leaves creates a truly scrap effect. Shirley Prescott used a different green fabric for each piece of the leaves plus a different brown fabric for each piece of the alternating leaves. The resulting quilt is not as clearly defined as the In the Red quilt on page 67 but appears quite random and almost abstract in appearance.

FABRIC REQUIREMENTS

Thirty-six blocks are needed for the Tumbling Leaves lap quilt – eighteen using set 1 fabrics and eighteen using set 2 fabrics.

◆ Set 1 fabrics (shades of green): 30in (76.1cm) of fabric in total 42in–44in (107cm–112cm) wide.

◆ Set 2 fabrics (shades of brown): 30in (76.1cm) of fabric in total 42in–44in (107cm–112cm) wide.

◆ Borders: inner – 14in (35.5cm) of fabric 42in–44in (107cm–112cm) wide;

middle – 4in (10cm) of fabric 42in–44in (107cm–112cm) wide

outer – 21in (53.3cm) of fabric 42in–44in (107cm–112cm) wide.

◆ Wadding and backing fabric: at least 2in (5cm) larger than finished quilt size.

Construction

For a truly random look this quilt uses as many different fabrics as possible from the set 1 green fabrics and the set 2 brown fabrics. The pieces of fabric to make one leaf can be cut from a rectangle of fabric measuring 9½in x 7in (24.1cm x 17.8cm) so a total of eighteen rectangles each 9½in x 7in (24.1cm x 17.8cm) must be cut from both set 1 and set 2 fabrics.

1 Cut every rectangle into the pieces as described in step 2 on page 68. Sort the cut pieces into piles of all the A pieces, all B pieces and so on. Follow steps 3–8 on page 68 to assemble eighteen blocks using set 1 fabrics, with a different fabric for each piece of the leaf design plus the two background pieces (D) from set 2 fabrics (Fig 15).

Fig 15

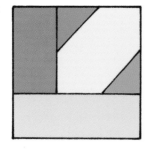

2 Repeat this process using the pieces from set 2 fabrics for the leaf design, each piece in a different fabric, plus the two background pieces from set 1 fabrics (Fig 16).

Fig 16

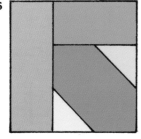

3 Arrange the thirty-six blocks in six rows with six blocks in each row as in Fig 17.

Fig 17

JOINING THE BLOCKS

Join the blocks together following the instructions given on page 70 in steps 3–6.

ADDING THE BORDERS

1 A simple border of dark green fabric cut 3½in (8.8cm) wide was used for the inner border. For the middle border, piece together all the little cut-off triangles from the blocks, a main fabric with a background, to make seventy-two squares. Press the seams to one side and trim each pieced square to exactly 1¾in x 1¾in (4.4cm x 4.4cm) (Fig 18).

Fig 18

2 Join the squares together in four lengths each of twelve squares and four lengths each of six squares. Take care to arrange the pieced squares exactly as shown in Fig 19.

Fig 19

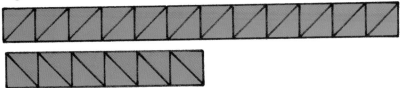

3 Cut four strips of a background fabric each strip measuring 1¾in x 20in (4.4cm x 50.8cm).

4 Stitch a length of twelve squares to a background strip. Join a length of six squares to the other end of the strip (Fig 20). Repeat this to make three more lengths.

Fig 20

5 Pin and stitch two of these fabric lengths to the sides of the quilt (Fig 21). Press the seams out away from the quilt.

6 Add two squares of background fabric, each cut 1¾in x 1¾in (4.4cm x 4.4cm), to either end of the two remaining border strips. Press

the seams inwards towards the border strips. Pin and stitch these to the top and bottom of the quilt (Fig 22).

7 The outer border is cut from another main fabric 3½in (8.8cm) wide. Bind the quilt in one of the main fabrics or with a multi-fabric binding. See Binding a Quilt on page 133.

QUILTING

Shirley quilted by machine ¼in (6mm) within each leaf to give emphasis to the leaf shapes in the design.

Fig 21

Fig 22

Scrap Lattice

The two very different quilts in this section show how versatile this simple block is. Debbie Langstaff has used it with a restrained colour palette to create an elegant and stylish quilt with careful use of light and dark tones (opposite). The 5in (12.7cm) square finished block is a perfect design for using up scraps. Two teams of fabric are used on two corners of a larger square of the main fabric or team of fabrics. The large square creates the diagonal lattice effect, with the corner triangles making the squares on point in between. Julia Reed's Batik Lattice quilt on page 81 (instructions on page 80) uses her favourite vibrant batiks to give a completely different effect to the design.

Elegant Lattice

Finished block size 5in x 5in (12.7cm x 12.7cm)
Finished quilt size 76in x 96in (193cm x 243.8cm)

THE QUILT STORY

Debbie Langstaff used her collection of cream/beige fabrics for the main lattice with stronger blues and browns as the corners (see picture opposite). The blues and browns have become the dominant element in the design with the cream/beige lattice as the background. The quilt is cool and elegant, typical of Debbie's work.

FABRIC REQUIREMENTS

For the Elegant Lattice quilt one set of fabrics that blend together is used for the diagonal lattice in the design plus two different sets for the triangular corners, which combine to make the squares on point. Use as many fabrics in each set as possible to achieve a scrap look.

◆ The lattice needs a total of 5½yd (5m) of assorted fabrics:

1½yd (1.37m) of set A fabrics for a triangular corner on each block (252 blocks);

1¼yd (1.15m) of set B fabrics for a triangular corner on 192 blocks.

◆ Border: 30in (76.2cm) of fabric for a 3in (7.6cm) finished width.

◆ Binding: ½yd (0.5m) of fabric.

◆ Wadding and backing fabric: at least 2in (5cm) larger than finished quilt size.

The initial cutting is all squares, which are then stitched together to make the block (Fig 1). The quilt design is simply the block repeated and stitched into units of four. A quick classic!

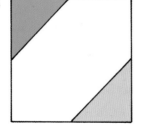

Fig 1

" It all started from a box of blue, a box of brown and a box of cream scraps from previous quilts. I thought of a throw to stop the cat scratching the sofa. The scraps made a lovely quilt so I am now decorating a room to match!
(Debbie Langstaff)

BITS AND PIECES QUILTS

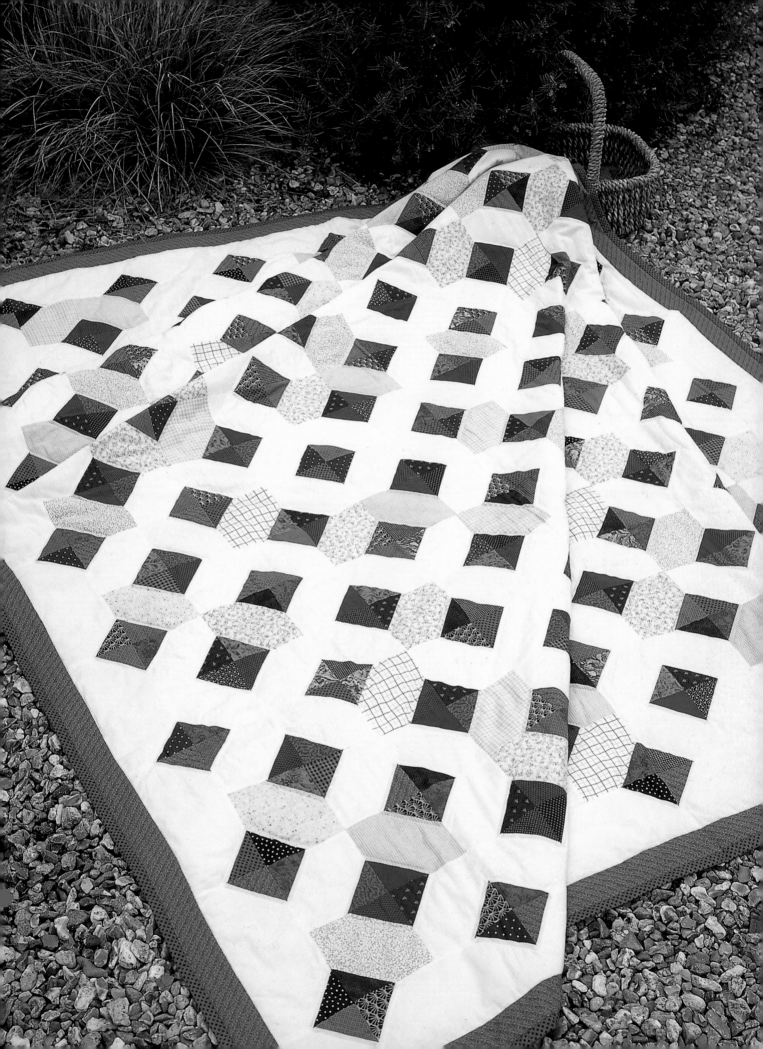

Construction

MAKING THE BLOCKS

1 From the fabrics to be used as the lattice in the quilt cut squares each measuring 5½in x 5½in (14cm x 14cm) – 252 squares are needed for the quilt, so use as many different fabrics as possible from the set that you have collected.

2 From each of the other two sets of fabric (A and B) that will make the triangular corners of the block cut squares measuring 3in x 3in (7.6cm x 7.6cm) – 252 of these are needed from set A and 192 from set B.

3 Place one smaller square of fabric from set A on to a corner of a large square, right sides together. Match the edges carefully and then pin in position (Fig 2).

Fig 2

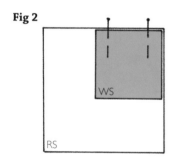

4 Stitch across the pinned square diagonally from corner to corner (Fig 3). To make the line to be stitched draw a line diagonally on the *wrong* side of the small fabric square with a marking pencil (see also the advice in the panel right).

Fig 3

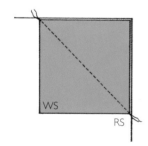

SEWING DIAGONALLY WITHOUT MARKING A GUIDELINE

To sew diagonally across a square of fabric without marking a guideline, stick a strip of masking tape on to the plate of the sewing machine with one edge level with the needle (Fig 4). Place the corner of the fabric to be stitched under the needle and position the opposite corner of the fabric exactly on top of the edge of the masking tape (Fig 5). Keep the bottom corner positioned on the edge of the masking tape at all times as you stitch the fabric.

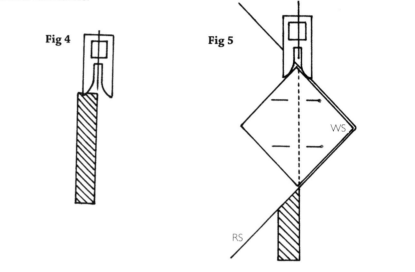

5 Trim the excess fabric ¼in (6mm) beyond the stitching line (Fig 6). The trimmed corners could be used later in a smaller design. Press back the triangle of fabric to make the corner of the square block, ironing from the front and pressing the seam out towards the corner (Fig 7).

Fig 6

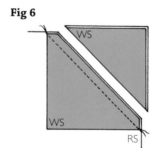

Fig 7

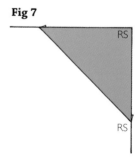

BITS AND PIECES QUILTS

6 Pin and stitch a small square from the other set of fabrics to the *opposite* corner of the large square in the same way (Fig 8).

Fig 8

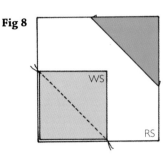

7 Trim the seam allowance as before and press back the triangle of fabric to make the corner of the square. This completes the block (Fig 9).

Fig 9

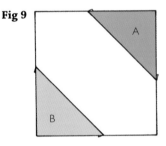

8 Continue to make these simple blocks, varying the fabrics as much as possible until 192 are completed. Set aside the remaining 60 squares without adding another corner to them.

ARRANGING AND JOINING THE BLOCKS

1 Take four of the double-cornered blocks and arrange them as in Fig 10. Grouping the blocks in fours makes the final assembling of the quilt easier to handle. The triangles of set A fabrics should all be placed in the centre of the design with the triangles from set B at the outer corners.

Fig 10

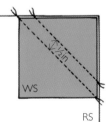

2 Pin and stitch together the top two blocks, matching seams carefully. Press the seam to one side, ironing from the front of the work.

3 Pin and stitch the bottom two blocks. Press the seam in the *opposite* direction to the top row. Finally pin and stitch the two rows together, matching seams carefully. Press the long seam to one side from the front of the work.

4 Using Fig 10 as a guide, continue to arrange and stitch four double-cornered blocks together to make a total of thirty-five large blocks. These blocks make the quilt centre. The large blocks around the edge of the quilt have a different arrangement as they include the small blocks that only have one corner replaced with set A fabric.

5 Arrange and stitch together two double-cornered blocks and two single-cornered blocks as in Fig 11 to make a total of twenty-four large blocks to be used as the outer edges of the quilt.

Fig 11

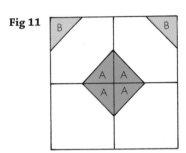

6 Arrange and stitch together one double-cornered block and three single-cornered blocks as in Fig 12 to make a total of four large blocks for the corners of the quilt.

Fig 12

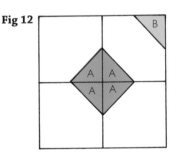

There are so many of those cut-off triangles that it seems a pity to just set them aside. They could make a wonderful quilt border by taking each pair of cut-off triangles and stitching them together along the diagonal sides to make a square. If you decide to do this *before* the corners are trimmed off, there is a clever way to join those corners into a square. Simply sew a second line of machine stitching parallel to the original stitching line but ½in (1.2cm) away from it, nearer the corner of the block. When the corners are trimmed ¼in (6mm) beyond the original stitching line (step 6), the two triangles that make the corner are already stitched together to make a square ready for use.

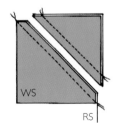

7 Arrange the blocks made from the design in Fig 10 in rows, five blocks in each row and seven rows down (Fig 13). Now place all the blocks from Fig 11 around the outer edges of the quilt with the four blocks from Fig 12 at the four corners of the quilt (Fig 14). Take time to balance the different fabrics across the quilt at this stage. If possible pin the blocks on to a wall or design board so that you can balance the colours of the blocks effectively. If this is not possible, lay them on the floor and stand on a chair or steps to view the overall design from as far away as possible.

Fig 13

Fig 14

To see which fabrics stand out as more dominant than the others, half-close your eyes as you view the design. The strong tones will leap out at you and it is these that you need to spread around the quilt to help balance it visually.

8 Pin and stitch the top row of blocks together with the usual ¼in (6mm) seam. Press the seams all to one side, ironing from the front.

9 Pin and stitch the second row of blocks together as before. Press the seams in the opposite direction to those of row 1 – this means that when the long rows are joined the seams will lock together.

10 Continue to pin and stitch each row of blocks, pressing the seams in alternate directions to help lock them.

11 Now join the rows together, matching seams carefully. Press the long seams to one side from the front of the work.

ADDING THE BORDER

Debbie's quilt was framed with a brown fabric cut 3½in (8.9cm) wide and finishing 3in (7.6cm) wide (see Bordering a Quilt on page 128).

QUILTING

Debbie quilted her Elegant Lattice quilt by machine by simply outlining each blue and brown square on point ¼in (6mm) away from the outer edge. Sometimes less is definitely more. . .

Batik Lattice

THE QUILT STORY

In this very different looking quilt, Julia Reed used cerise/purple batiks as her colour set for the large squares that make the lattice design on the quilt. The triangular corners were composed of two strongly contrasting sets – one yellow/reds and the other turquoise/greens. The whole effect is well-balanced and very striking.

Finished block size 5in x 5in (12.7cm x 12.7cm)
Finished quilt size 57½in x 57½in (146cm x 146cm)

When using batiks, do not spend time agonizing about the changes in colour that occur in one half yard of fabric. This is the nature of these fabrics – just cut them up and use each piece regardless.

FABRIC REQUIREMENTS

For the Batik Lattice quilt, one set of fabrics that blend together is used for the diagonal lattice in the design, plus two different sets (A and B) for the triangular corners that combine to make the square on point. Use as many fabrics in each set as possible for a scrap look.

◆ The lattice needs a total of 2½yd (2.3m) of assorted fabrics:

  1¼yd (1.15m) of set A fabrics for a triangular corner on each block and for the narrow frame border;

  1½yd (1.37m) of set B fabrics for a triangular corner on each block and the final border and binding.

◆ Wadding and backing fabric: at least 2in (5cm) larger than finished quilt size.

Construction

MAKING THE BLOCKS

1 From the fabrics to be used as the lattice in the quilt cut squares each measuring 5½in x 5½in (14cm x 14cm) – 100 squares are needed for this Batik Lattice quilt so use as many different fabrics as possible from the set that you have collected.

2 From each of the other two sets of fabric (A and B), which will make the triangular corners of the block, cut squares measuring 3in x 3in (7.6cm x 7.6cm) – 100 of these from each of set A and set B are needed, one of each used in each block.

3 Follow steps 3–7 on page 76 to make the blocks and make 100 blocks in total.

ARRANGING AND JOINING THE BLOCKS

1 Follow steps 1–3 on page 77 to join the blocks into groups of four. Make sixteen of these larger blocks as in Fig 10 on page 77. Leave the remaining thirty-six small blocks alone for the moment.

2 Arrange the larger blocks into the central quilt design shown in Fig 15 – four blocks across and four blocks down. Take time to balance the different fabrics across the quilt. If possible pin the blocks on to a wall or design board so that you can balance the colours of the blocks effectively. If this is not possible, lay them on the floor and stand on a chair or steps to view the overall design from as far away as possible (see also the technique tip on page 78).

Fig 15

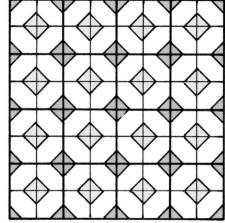

3 Follow steps 8–11 on page 79 to join the centre part of the quilt together.

When I was asked to make a bright version of this pattern I thought guiltily of my extensive batik stash and thought, 'Yes, I can do that!' (Julia Reed)

ADDING THE BORDERS

1 Julia used border frames and extra blocks to make a really effective border for her quilt (Fig 16). Join thirty-two of the remaining blocks into four lengths each of eight blocks as in Fig 17. Press the seams to one side, ironing from the front.

2 To make the narrow inner frame, cut strips from a mixture of set A fabrics, each 1½in (3.8cm) wide and in lengths varying from 4in–6in (10cm–15.2cm). Join these together in any order to make the following:

two strips 1½in x 40½in
(3.8cm x 102.9cm);

two strips 1½in x 52½in
(3.8cm x 133.4cm);

two strips 1½in x 5½in
(3.8cm x 14cm).

Fig 16

Fig 17

3 Pin and stitch each of the pieced strips measuring 40½in (102.9cm) (or your own quilt measurement) to a length of eight blocks in the exact arrangement shown in Fig 18. Press the seams from the front, towards the narrow border strip.

Fig 18

✂ Measure the pieced quilt centre – it should be 40½in (102.9cm) in both directions across its centre. The four lengths of eight joined blocks should also be 40½in (102.9cm). If this isn't the case, try to get the quilt and all four strips of joined blocks to measure the same as each other, either by re-stitching or by using a steam iron. Use this measurement as the length of the first two strips for the narrow frame. The longer two strips of the frame should measure this amount plus 12in (30.5cm). The two short strips remain unaltered.

✂ Continuing a pieced design beyond a framing border as Julia has done can present problems, as the additional border strip adds to the measurements of the quilt, which may then not be compatible with the measurements of the original piecing design. Julia solved this by continuing the border strips out to the edges of the quilt at the corners (see steps 3–7).

4 Pin and stitch these to either side of the quilt (Fig 19). Press seams towards the narrow border strip, ironing from the front.

Fig 19

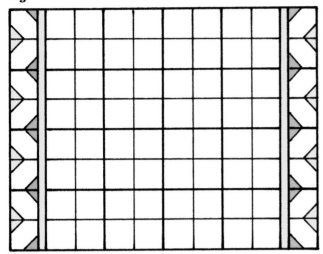

5 Pin and stitch first a short length of narrow border and then a pieced block to either end of each strip of eight blocks (Fig 20). Press the seams from the front towards the narrow border strip.

Fig 20

6 Pin and stitch a long narrow border strip to one long edge of each of these pieced lengths (Fig 21). Press the seams from the front, towards the narrow border strip.

Fig 21

> **!** Check that both narrow border strips are stitched along the bottom edge of each length of blocks, with the diagonal strips making exactly the same pattern as in Fig 21 each time. If the narrow border strip is stitched to the top edge the overall lattice design across the quilt will be lost.

7 Pin and stitch the two lengths to the top and bottom of the quilt, matching the crossroads of the narrow border strips carefully (Fig 22). Press the seams in towards the narrow border frame.

Fig 22

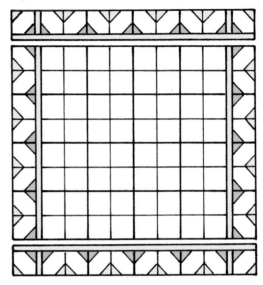

8 The final border is made from joined pieces of set B fabrics each cut 3in (7.6cm) wide and in lengths varying from 3in x 5in (7.6cm x 12.7cm) (see Bordering a Quilt on page 128). The quilt is bound with joined strips of the same set of fabrics.

QUILTING

Julia loves free-motion machine quilting and enjoyed doodling across her quilt with a freestyle design of leaves and flowers. How I wish I could do that!

Corner Square

One of my students, Mary Harrowell, chose this simple but effective corner square design when asked by the builder working on her house if she would make him a quilt. Aware that a reliable builder is to be prized above pearls she readily agreed. She made the quilt quickly, quilted it simply by machine and presented it to the delighted man. From then on in my classes this corner square design became known as a 'Bob the Builder' quilt. The repeated block is ideal for a scrap quilt, using up odd pieces of as many fabrics as possible, as you can see by Avril Ellis' quilt, opposite. The block is made from a corner square of dark fabric plus a large half-square triangle of medium-toned fabric. These two shapes are separated by two smaller half-square triangles of light fabric.

In Victorian Mood

Finished block size 5in x 5in (12.7cm x 12.7cm)
Finished quilt size 98in x 78in (249cm x 198cm)

THE QUILT STORY

Avril Ellis made her corner square quilt (opposite) with all the scraps of rich blues, browns, reds and yellows in her stash. She limited her colours to this range, omitting pinks and greens, to give a Victorian feel to the quilt, and used cream calico as the light triangles throughout. The complex plaited border was taken from Camille Remme's excellent book *Celtic Geometric Quilts*, an American Quilters' Society publication (1996). For the faint-hearted and those with a deadline to keep I have suggested simpler alternative borders in the instructions that follow.

FABRIC REQUIREMENTS

See overleaf for advice on choosing fabrics.

◆ For the corner squares in each block: about 2yd (2m) of assorted dark fabrics.

◆ For the large half-square triangles in each block: about 2½yd (2.3m) of assorted medium fabrics.

◆ Assorted light fabrics (or one background light fabric if preferred), about 2½yd (2.3m).

◆ Borders: 1st – 30in of a dark fabric, 3in (7.5cm) finished width;

further borders – a border 3in–4in (7.5cm–10cm) can be cut from 1yd (1m), while 1½yd (1.37m) would give a wider border with just one central join on each side.

◆ Binding: 21in (53.3cm) of fabric 42in–44in (106.7cm–111.8cm) wide.

◆ Wadding and backing fabric: at least 2in (5cm) larger than finished quilt size.

This quilt is made from just one simple block repeated as many times as necessary. Instead of cutting individual squares and triangles the blocks are made two at a time from strips in a quick and easy method.

"I am really pleased with my quilt although I admit I find the concept of making a design from random scraps very difficult. To overcome this I used shades of blue for one side of the large triangles and brown for the other. (Avril Ellis)"

Choosing the fabrics

You may wish to use everything you have in your stash or do a preliminary sort at the start to restrict colours so the quilt is more co-ordinated. Once you have made your selection the fabrics need to be sorted into three piles. The first is for the dark squares in each block (see Fig 1). These run through the quilt 'floating' on the light triangles, so need to be of a similar colour strength. The second pile is of medium tones to make the large half-square triangles in the block. The final group should be either one light fabric or a collection of very similar fabrics – in this way the dark and medium areas are kept separate and have more impact in the design.

Fig 1

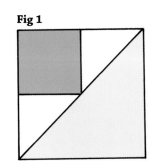

Construction

✂ **Strips that are cut in the same direction as the selvedge or woven edge will be far less stretchy and therefore easier to handle than strips cut across the fabric from selvedge to selvedge. If you have to use strips cut across the fabric, be aware that they tend to stretch and do not pull on them as you stitch. Alternatively, spray-starch the fabric pieces before you cut the strips to keep them firmer.**

Cutting the fabric

1 From the dark fabrics cut strips 3in (7.6cm) wide. As a large number of fabrics are being used, cut just one strip from each, no more than 18in–20in (45.7cm–50.8cm) long. This will give five or six corner squares to use in the quilt – thirty-nine strips will be enough for all 192 blocks used in Avril's quilt. (This may seem like a huge number but they are made really quickly and make up the whole quilt design, so there's nothing else apart from borders to wrestle with – honestly. . .)

2 From the light fabrics (or one light background fabric if preferred) cut strips 4in (10cm) wide. Again, cut these into 18in–20in (45.7cm–50.8cm) lengths to match the dark strips – thirty-nine strips will be needed.

3 From the medium fabrics cut rectangles 5½in x 6½in (14cm x 16.5cm). These will make the large half-square triangles in each block: one square will make two blocks, so ninety-six rectangles are needed for the quilt. Vary the fabrics as much as possible.

Making the block

4 Take one cut strip of dark fabric and one cut strip of light fabric. Stitch the strips together with right sides facing, using a ¼in (6mm) seam allowance and a smaller stitch than for dress-making. Press the seam from the front *towards* the light fabric (Fig 2).

Fig 2

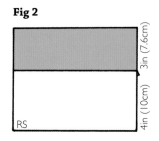

! Yes, you have read this correctly – the seam is pressed *towards* the light fabric. Not usual in most patchwork techniques, but essential here because it makes the construction of the blocks easier and keep seams flatter.

5 Now repeat this process with a different dark strip and background light strip.

6 Cut each pair of stitched strips into pieces each 3in (7.6cm) wide (Fig 3).

Fig 3

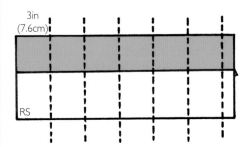

7 Arrange two different cut pieces as in Fig 4 and then pin and stitch them together (Fig 5).

Fig 4   **Fig 5**

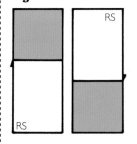

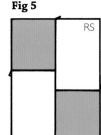

8 Mark the long seam at its centre, i.e., 3¼in (8.3cm) along the seam. Cut the seam allowance carefully at this point at right angles to the line of stitching (Fig 6). Do not cut the stitching itself, but cut as close up to it as you safely can. Open the block and press the top section of the seam allowance *towards* the light fabric, ironing from the front of the work. Press the lower half of the seam allowance also towards the lighter fabric (Fig 7).

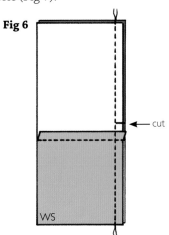

Fig 6

← cut

WS

Fig 7

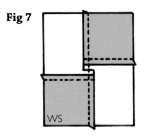

WS

9 Place the block right side *down* on a flat surface. Take a square ruler and place it on the block with its diagonal marking on the edge of the block as in Fig 8. The top corner of the ruler should meet the edge of the block 1in (2.5cm) from the top left corner of the block and cross the bottom right corner exactly. The diagonal edge of the ruler should also hit the inner corner of the lower stitched square of the block. Draw a line on the block along the diagonal edge of the ruler with a marking pencil (Fig 9).

Fig 8

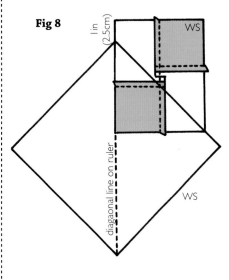

1in (2.5cm)

WS

diagaonal line on ruler

WS

Fig 9

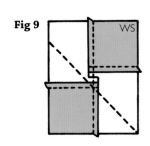

WS

10 Turn the block 180 degrees. Place the ruler on the opposite corner of the block as before and draw along the diagonal edge (Fig 10).

Fig 10

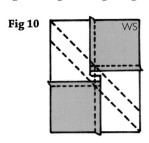

WS

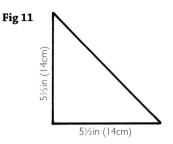
11 Place the pieced block on to a cut piece of medium fabric, 5½in x 6½in (14cm x 16.5cm), right sides facing. Match edges carefully. Pin together and stitch along both pencil lines (Fig 12).

Fig 12

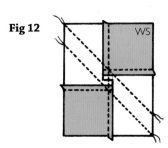

WS

12 Cut the block in half, cutting between the stitched diagonal lines (Fig 13).

Fig 13

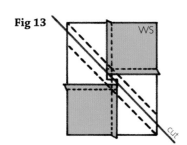

13 Open out each half and press the seam to one side, ironing from the front. You should now have two blocks, each measuring 5½in x 5½in (14cm x 14cm).

14 Before making any more blocks you will need more dark squares to choose from rather than repeating the fabrics of the two blocks you have just made. Stitch together and press all the remaining dark and light strips and cut a few pieces from each pair ready to use in the blocks (steps 4–6 on page 86).

15 Follow steps 7–13 to make as many blocks as are needed for your project. Avril's In Victorian Mood quilt needed 192 blocks in total.

Fig 14

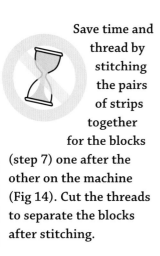

Save time and thread by stitching the pairs of strips together for the blocks (step 7) one after the other on the machine (Fig 14). Cut the threads to separate the blocks after stitching.

ARRANGING AND JOINING THE BLOCKS

1 Avril arranged her blocks in a simple diagonal but there are many other arrangements possible, so enjoy playing with the blocks before you come to a final decision and stitch them together. Two different arrangements are shown in Fig 15 (on the opposite page).

2 Once the final arrangement is made, pin and stitch the top row of twelve blocks together with the usual ¼in (6mm) seam. Press the seams to one side, ironing from the front.

3 Pin and stitch the second row of blocks together. Press seams in the opposite direction to those of row 1, ironing from the front. Continue to pin and stitch each row, pressing seams in alternate directions to help lock them.

4 Join the rows together, matching seams carefully. Press seams to one side from the front.

ADDING THE BORDERS

If you wish to make the complex border on Avril's quilt see page 84 for details of the book source. As an alternative I suggest a simpler border of three frames (Fig 16) or one that uses leftover dark squares from the blocks as one of the frames (Fig 17).

Fig 16

alternate border

Fig 17

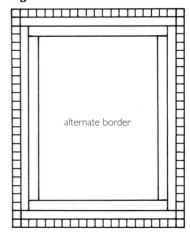

alternate border

For a triple-frame quilt (Fig 16), the inner border of dark fabric is cut 3½in (8.9cm) wide. The middle border of light background fabric is cut 3in (7.6cm) wide and the outer frame of a different dark fabric is cut 4in (10cm) wide. (See Bordering a Quilt page 128.)

For the alternative design (Fig 17) the inner border is cut 3½in (8.9cm) wide. The second border of light background fabric is cut 2½in (6.4cm). The outer border uses squares of dark fabric leftovers from the quilt blocks each cut 3in x 3in (7.6cm x 7.6cm). The final binding for both versions could be in a dark fabric.

QUILTING

Avril quilted the main central design by machine in a series of gently curving lines that flow diagonally across the quilt and echo the diagonal arrangement of the piecing design. The geometric border was edged with machine quilting ¼in (6mm) away from the interlocking strips.

Fig 15
Two alternative
arrangements

Star and Nine-Patch

The two blocks featured in this section are both based on 3in (7.6cm) finished squares and complement each other well. One is a simple Nine-Patch block made from just two fabrics (Fig 1 below), while the other is a Star Nine-Patch block, where the star 'floats' on a background fabric (Fig 2). Different arrangements of these two blocks are shown in two quilts by Marianne Bennett. In her Classic Gold scrap quilt (opposite) light Star blocks alternate with darker Nine-Patch blocks to give a traditional feel. On page 101, in her Star Bright version, she placed all the Star blocks in the centre area floating on a black background, surrounding them with brightly coloured nine-patches. Both quilts have the blocks arranged on point to give a more interesting design. The complex pieced borders could be replaced with a series of simple frames if preferred.

Classic Gold

Finished block size 9in x 9in (22.9cm x 22.9cm)
Finished quilt size 97in x 97in (246.4cm x 246.4cm)

THE QUILT STORY

During my regular classes in Chelsworth in Suffolk I had demonstrated a quick and clever technique for making two Nine-Patch blocks at once, using the same two fabrics and reversing the arrangement in the second block. Some while later I showed another easily constructed Nine-Patch block, a Star Nine-Patch. Marianne decided to combine the two blocks and used her pile of Civil War reproduction fabrics to make the classic quilt opposite in a range of warm and wonderful golds, browns and creams.

FABRIC REQUIREMENTS

◆ You will need an assortment of fabrics that look good together as the Nine-Patch blocks and the Star blocks, as many as possible – about 6½yd (6m) in total. These are also used as the squares in the second border.

◆ 3yd (2.75m) of background fabric for Star blocks and edging triangles around blocks.

◆ ½yd (0.5m) of fabric for the inner lighter triangles in the second border.

◆ 1yd (1m) for the outer triangles in the second border plus the binding.

◆ Wadding and backing fabric: at least 2in (5cm) larger than finished quilt size.

" I love quilts that have the blocks arranged on point, so this is what I did with the two different Nine-Patch blocks in my quilt. I was going to make it smaller with a simple frame border but it just seemed to need the pieced border instead, which made it huge! (Marianne Bennett)"

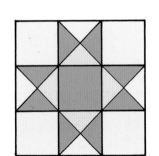

Fig 1   **Fig 2**

BITS AND PIECES QUILTS

Construction

MAKING THE NINE-PATCH BLOCKS

Individual scrap Nine-Patch blocks are usually made by cutting individual squares and stitching them together row by row. This speedier method starts with two squares of fabric and finishes with two Nine-Patch blocks, one a reverse arrangement of the other (Fig 3).

The design combines two different Nine-Patch blocks, both of which are made with extra quick and sneaky techniques.

Fig 3

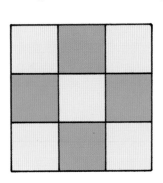

1 Choose two fabrics that will look good together in the block and from each cut one square measuring 10½in x 10½in (26.7cm x 26.7cm).

2 Place the squares together with right sides facing, lining up the edges exactly. Using a smaller stitch than for dressmaking, stitch a ¼in (6mm) seam down both sides (Fig 4).

Fig 4

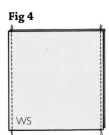

3 Use a rotary cutter and ruler to cut the layered squares vertically into three equal strips, each measuring 3½in (8.9cm) in width (Fig 5).

Fig 5

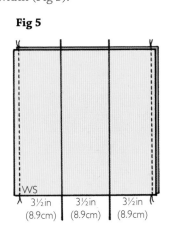

3½in (8.9cm) 3½in (8.9cm) 3½in (8.9cm)

4 Open out each of the two stitched pairs of fabric and place one of the single cut strips with it, as in Fig 6.

Fig 6

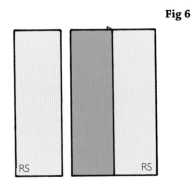
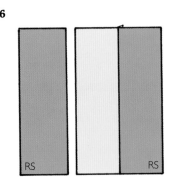

5 Pin and stitch the single strip to each pair of fabric strips. Press the seams towards the darker fabric, ironing from the front of the work (Fig 7).

Fig 7

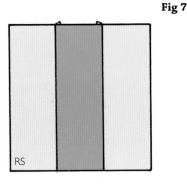
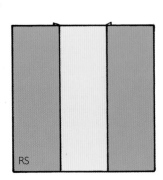

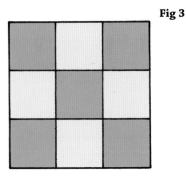

BITS AND PIECES QUILTS

Measure the stitched blocks from side to side across the centre – they should both measure 9½in (24.1cm). If this is not the case, now is the time to adjust your ¼in (6mm) seam allowance to get this right.

6 Turn the blocks so that the seams are running horizontally as in Fig 8. Place the two pieced blocks together with right sides facing, matching the seams and lining up the outer edges as accurately as possible. The seams of both blocks should be lying on top of each other.

Fig 8

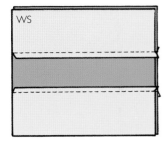

7 Pin the side edges, especially at the matched seams, before stitching the side seams as before (Fig 9).

Fig 9

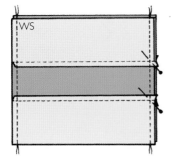

Pin the matched seams diagonally (Fig 10). This will help to keep both seam allowances flat while stitching.

Fig 10

8 Cut the stitched squares vertically into three strips as before, each strip measuring 3½in (8.9cm) wide (Fig 11).

Fig 11

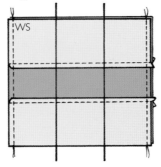

9 Open out each of the stitched pairs of strips and place one of the single cut strips with it in the arrangements shown in Fig 12.

10 Pin and stitch the single strips to the joined pairs of strips, matching seams carefully. Press the seams towards the centre of the block, ironing from the front. The two Nine-Patch blocks are now complete.

11 Choose another pair of fabrics from the collection that you feel will combine well in a nine-patch. Cut two squares each 10½in x 10½in (26.7cm x 26.7cm) and follow steps 2–10 to make two more Nine-Patch blocks. For this classic quilt twenty-five Nine-Patch blocks are needed (you will have one left over as a spare).

This method of making two Nine-Patch blocks at once from large squares of fabric is ideal for making miniature quilts. To calculate the size needed, first decide on the final size of each square in the Nine-patch block. Add the seam allowance to this and multiply this measurement by three (because there are three squares in each row in the Nine-Patch block). For example, for finished 1in (2.5cm) squares, add ½in (1.2cm) for the seam allowance (1½in/3.8cm) and multiply by three. This equals 4½in (11.4cm), which is the size of square in each fabric that you need to start with.

Fig 12

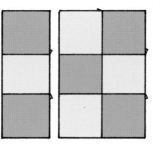

MAKING THE STAR BLOCKS

For the Classic Gold quilt each block uses two fabrics for the star plus a background fabric which is used in every Star block.

1 From the fabric marked A in the block (see Fig 13) cut one square measuring 4¼in x 4¼in (10.8cm x 10.8cm).

From the fabric marked B cut two squares measuring 4¼in x 4¼in (10.8cm x 10.8cm) plus one square 3½in x 3½in (8.9cm x 8.9cm) for the centre.

From the background fabric marked C cut four squares measuring 3½in x 3½in (8.9cm x 8.9cm) plus one square 4¼in x 4¼in (10.8cm x 10.8cm).

Fig 13

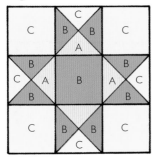

2 Take two cut squares of fabric B each measuring 4¼in (10.8cm). Draw a diagonal line on the wrong side of each fabric square, using a sharp marking pencil (Fig 14).

Fig 14

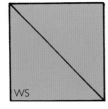

3 Place one of these with right sides facing on to the 4¼in (10.8cm) square of fabric A and the other on to the 4¼in (10.8cm) square of the background fabric C. Match the edges carefully and pin together.

4 Machine a line of stitching on either side of the drawn diagonal line at a distance of exactly ¼in (6mm) (Fig 15). (See the useful tip below.)

Fig 15

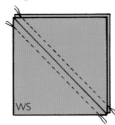

To machine a line on either side of a drawn line at exactly ¼in (6mm) try the following:
a) use a special ¼in (6mm) foot on the machine;
b) if your machine has the facility, move the needle until the distance between it and the side of your usual machine foot is exactly ¼in (6mm);
c) draw in a stitching line ¼in (6mm) away from the diagonal line on both sides, using a different colour marking pencil to avoid confusion.

5 Cut along the drawn line on each stitched square. Open out the stitched triangles to make four squares (Fig 16). Press the seams from the front towards fabric B. Trim the seam allowances back level with the edges

of the square. Each square should now measure 3⅞in (9.8cm) – if yours does not, you need to adjust your ¼in (6mm) seam allowance.

Fig 16

To correct squares that are too big, trim them to the correct size. Use a square ruler and match the diagonal line on the ruler with the diagonal seam on the fabric square as you trim. For squares that are too small, re-stitch the diagonal seam with a narrower seam allowance before removing the original stitching.

6 Take the two pieced squares made from fabrics A and B and draw a diagonal line on the wrong side of each square as in Fig 17.

Fig 17

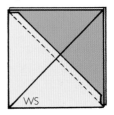

7 Place one of these marked squares on to each of the other two pieced squares with right sides facing and edges matching. The diagonal seams should be lying exactly on top of each other. Because the seam allowances are pressed in opposite directions, the seams should butt together nicely. Pin the squares together.

8 Stitch a ¼in (6mm) seam on either side of the drawn lines as before (Fig 18).

Fig 18

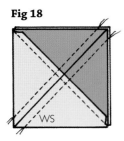

9 Cut along the drawn diagonal line on each stitched square. Open out the stitched triangles to make four squares as in Fig 19. Press the seams to one side from the front.

Fig 19

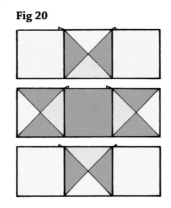

10 Trim the seam allowance level with the edges of each square, which should measure 3½in x 3½in (8.9cm x 8.9cm). If this is a problem, follow the technique tip above step 6 to adjust the size.

11 Arrange the four pieced squares with the four corner background squares and the one centre square to make the star design as shown in Fig 13.

12 Pin and stitch together the top row of three squares. Press seams towards the background squares, ironing from the front of the work.

13 Pin and stitch together the middle row of squares, pressing the seams towards the centre square of the star design. Stitch together the third row of squares. Press the seams towards the background squares (Fig 20). This way

the seams will lie flatter and will lock together neatly when the three rows are joined.

Fig 20

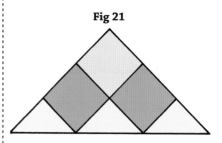

14 Stitch the three rows together, matching seams carefully. Press the seams away from the centre of the block, ironing from the front.

15 Continue to make Star blocks following steps 1–14 each time (beginning on page 94). For the Classic Gold quilt make thirty-six Star blocks.

ASSEMBLING THE QUILT

In addition to the twenty-five Nine-Patch blocks and thirty-six Star blocks that are arranged on point, triangular edging units (a in Fig 22) are needed to fill in the gaps around the blocks. Marianne used squares and triangles of her fabrics to piece these units (Fig 21). Twenty pieced units are needed to edge the quilt, five along each side, plus four smaller pieced triangular units (b) for the corners of the quilt.

Fig 21

Fig 22

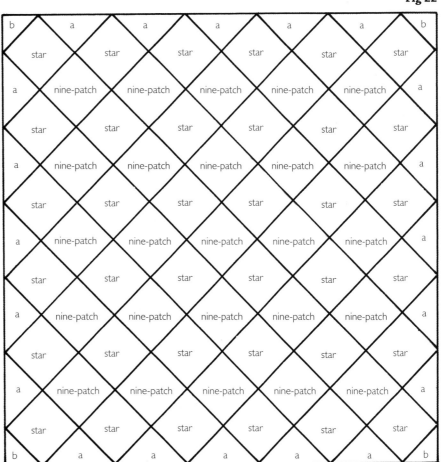

Making the triangular edging units (a)

1 From the fabrics used for the Nine-Patch blocks cut sixty squares each measuring 3½in x 3½in (8.9cm x 8.9cm). From the background fabric cut thirty squares each 3⅞in x 3⅞in (9.8cm x 9.8cm). Cut each square diagonally into two triangles.

2 Now arrange three squares and three triangles into three rows as shown in Fig 23.

Fig 23

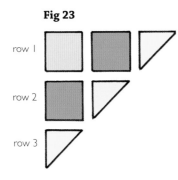

3 Stitch the top row together with a ¼in (6mm) seam. Press the seams to one side, ironing from the front. Stitch the second row together. Press the seams in the opposite direction to row 1. Pin and stitch rows 1 and 2 together (Fig 24). Finally, add the triangle of row 3 to complete the triangular block as in Fig 21. Repeat this process to make all the edging triangular units (a total of twenty).

Fig 24

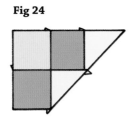

Making the triangular corner units (b)

4 From the nine-patch fabrics cut four squares each 3½in x 3½in (8.9cm x 8.9cm). From the background fabric cut four squares each 3⅞in x 3⅞in (9.8cm x 9.8cm) and two squares each 3in x 3in (7.6cm x 7.6cm). Cut each square of background fabric diagonally into two triangles.

5 Pin and stitch together one square and two of the larger triangles (Fig 25). Press the seams away from the square. Pin and stitch one of the smaller triangles to the top of the block (Fig 26). Press the seams away from the square.

Fig 25

Fig 26

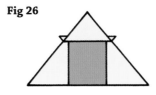

6 Repeat this process to make all four corner triangular units.

7 Arrange the blocks and edging triangles as in Fig 22.

8 The design is pinned and stitched in diagonal rows (see Fig 27, opposite page). Begin with row 1, pinning and stitching the three pieces together as in Fig 28. Press seams towards the edging triangles, ironing from the front.

Fig 28

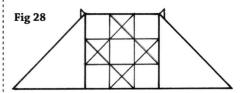

9 Pin and stitch row 2 together, pressing seams away from the Star blocks. Continue to pin and stitch together rows 3–11, following Fig 27 for positioning the edging triangles on each row. Press the seams away from the Star blocks each time, ironing from the front.

10 Stitch the rows together row by row, matching seams carefully. Finally, add the four corner blocks to complete the design. If necessary trim the outer edges of the quilt to make them all level with each other.

BORDERING THE QUILT

The inner border is a simple frame of strips cut 4½in (11.4cm) wide. The middle pieced border is made from four-patch squares turned on point and edged with triangles in a Seminole-type design (Fig 29). The final border is of the same fabric as the inner border but cut 4in (10cm) wide (see Bordering a Quilt page 128). The quilt was bound with the dark fabric used for the triangles in the middle border.

Fig 29

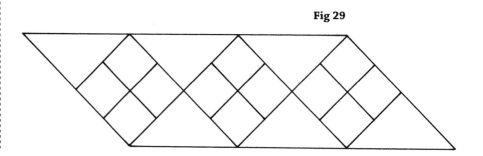

Fig 27

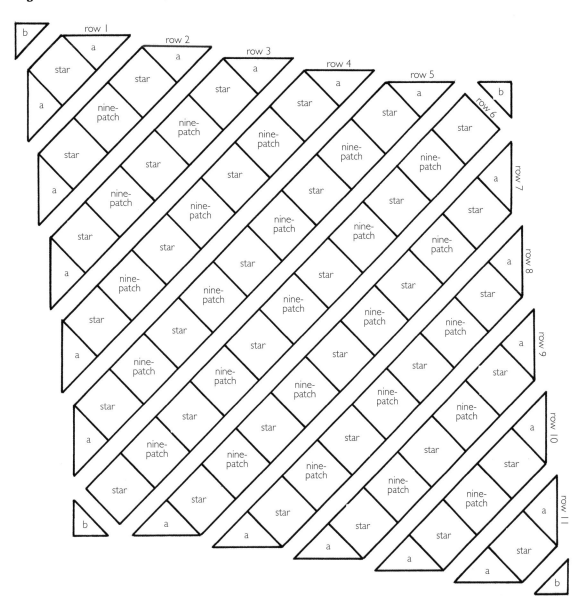

Piecing the middle border

1 From fabric left over from the blocks cut one strip of light fabric and one of dark fabric each 2¼in x 5in (5.7cm x 12.7cm). Stitch these together with a ¼in (6mm) seam. Press the seam towards the darker strip (Fig 30a).

2 Cut the strip vertically into two pieces, each measuring 2¼in (5.7cm) wide (Fig 30b).

3 Turn the second piece round through 180 degrees. Pin and stitch the two pieces together to make a four-patch, matching the centre seams carefully (Fig 30c). Press the seam to one side, ironing from the front.

Fig 30a

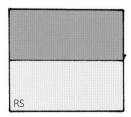

RS

Fig 30b

2¼in (5.7cm) 2¼in (5.7cm)

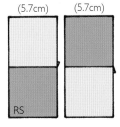

RS

Fig 30c

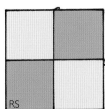

RS

4 Make a total of sixty-four of these Four-Patch blocks from as many different fabrics as possible, always combining a light and a dark fabric.

5 From the fabric chosen for the inner lighter triangles, cut thirty squares each measuring 4⅜in (11cm). From the outer darker fabric cut thirty-four squares each measuring 4⅜in (11cm). Cut both sets of squares in half diagonally to make triangles.

6 Pin and stitch a triangle of each fabric to opposite sides of each four-patch as in Fig 31.

Fig 31

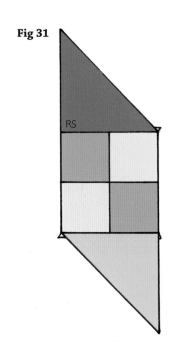

> **Make sure that each Four-Patch block is arranged in exactly the same way each time. The dark squares should always be in the same position or the overall pattern of lights and darks will be lost.**

7 Pin and stitch two pieced units together, stepping the second piece down as in Fig 32 and matching the seams carefully. Press the seam to one side.

Fig 32

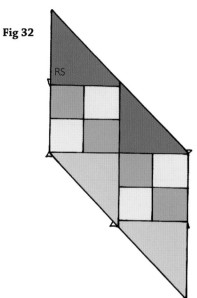

8 Join fifteen pieces together in this way to make the strips for one side. Make four of these strips.

9 An extra, different unit is needed on one end of each strip to make the four corners fit together. To the four remaining Four-Patch blocks pin and stitch two dark triangles in the arrangement in Fig 33. Stitch these on to one end of each strip as in Fig 34.

Fig 33

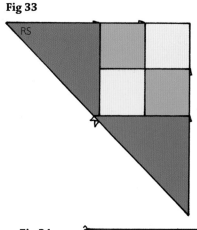

10 Mark the turning corner of the seamline at each corner of the quilt with a pencilled dot on the wrong side (Fig 35a). Do the same at either end of each border strip (Fig 35b).

Fig 35a

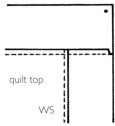

quilt top

WS

Fig 35b

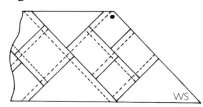

WS

11 Pin each border strip to the sides of the quilt, matching the corner dots. Stitch the strips in place, starting and finishing exactly at the marked dots each time.

Fig 34

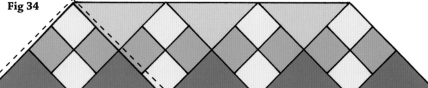

extra unit

BITS AND PIECES QUILTS

12 Finally, pin and stitch the corner diagonal seams, matching the seams carefully (Fig 36). Press these four seams open to help the mitred corners to lie flat.

Fig 36

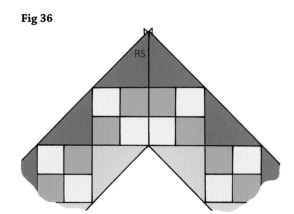

RS

QUILTING

Marianne machine quilted her Classic Gold quilt in simple straight lines across the quilt blocks, in order that the quilting did not distract too much from the formal arrangement of the blocks.

Consider using the four-patch border described on pages 97 and 98 as a border around a completely different quilt project in the future. It is such a stunning design that it deserves to be seen in more than one quilt.

Star Bright

THE QUILT STORY

After Marianne had completed her Classic Gold quilt (previously described on pages 90–99) she then used a stash of wild fabrics plus black in a different interpretation of the design, finishing as the Star Bright quilt opposite. No two quilts could be more different! How Marianne could have possessed both collections in her stash I do not know – it just proves how unpredictable the lust to acquire fabric can be.

Finished block size
9in x 9in (22.9cm x 22.9cm)
Finished quilt size
97in x 97in (246.4cm x 246.4cm)

FABRIC REQUIREMENTS

◆ You will need an assortment of fabrics that look good together as the Nine-Patch blocks and the Star blocks, as many as possible – about 6½yd (6m) in total. These are also used as the squares in the second border.

◆ 3yd (2.75m) of background fabric for Star blocks and the edging triangles around the blocks.

◆ Borders: ½yd (0.5m) of fabric for the first and third borders. An extra ¾yd (0.7m) of background fabric, plus leftover squares from the Nine-Patch blocks for the middle border. For fabric quantities for simpler framing borders see page 128.

◆ ½yd (0.5m) for the final binding on the quilt.

◆ Wadding and backing fabric: at least 2in (5cm) larger than the finished quilt size.

Construction

MAKING THE NINE-PATCH BLOCKS

Beginning on page 92, follow steps 1–11 for making the Nine-Patch blocks. For this Star Bright quilt thirty-six Nine-Patch blocks should be made.

MAKING THE STAR BLOCKS

Each Star block in this quilt uses two fabrics for the star and sometimes a third fabric for the centre square. A black background fabric is used in every Star block (Fig 13, page 94). Follow the instructions for making the Star block in the Classic Gold quilt (steps 1–14 from page 94).

If you want a different fabric for the centre square, do not cut this from fabric B but choose a new fabric for this square. Make twenty-five Star blocks in total for this bright quilt.

ASSEMBLING THE QUILT

In addition to the thirty-six Nine-Patch blocks and twenty-five Star blocks that are arranged on point, edging triangles of background fabric are needed to fill in the gaps around the blocks. Twenty triangles are needed to edge the quilt, five along each side, plus four smaller triangles for the corners of the quilt (Fig 37).

Fig 37

“ *I used my computer to play with the arrangements of these really bright blocks. The choice of the background marbled black fabric helped to control the brightness a little – I think! (Marianne Bennett)* ”

Cutting the larger edging triangles (a)

1 From the background fabric cut five squares each 14in x 14in (35.6cm x 35.6cm). Cut each square into four diagonally (Fig 38) to give a total of twenty triangles.

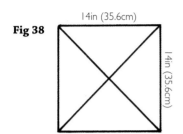

Fig 38

14in (35.6cm)

14in (35.6cm)

Cutting the four smaller corner triangles (b)

2 From the background fabric cut two squares each 7¼in x 7¼in (18.4cm x 18.4cm). Cut each square in half diagonally.

If you are unable to cut five large 14in (35.6cm) squares from the fabric, draw the triangle in Fig 39 accurately on graph paper and stick it on card to make a template. Use this template to draw round and cut out twenty large triangles (seam allowances included). Be careful to match the grain line arrow on the template with the fabric weave.

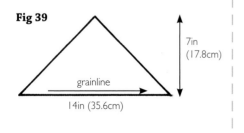

Fig 39

7in (17.8cm)

grainline

14in (35.6cm)

3 Arrange the blocks and edging triangles as in Fig 37 (previous page). The design is pinned and stitched in diagonal rows (Fig 40).

Fig 40

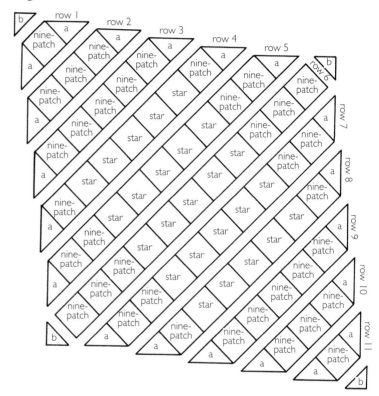

4 Begin with row 1, pinning and stitching the three pieces together as in Fig 41. Press seams away from the Nine-Patch block.

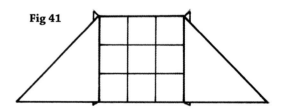

Fig 41

5 Pin and stitch row 2 together, pressing seams in the opposite direction to row 1. Continue to pin and stitch together rows 3–11, following Fig 40 for positioning the edging triangles on each row. Press the seams of each row in alternate directions to help to lock them.

6 Stitch the rows together row by row, matching seams carefully. Finally, add the two corner blocks to complete the design. If necessary trim the edges of the quilt to make them all level with each other.

ADDING THE BORDER

Marianne created a one-off original border for this quilt, playing with odd squares on point and generally having a good time. She also had no idea afterwards just how she had done it – creativity run wild! There was no way we could document this for general instructions so I suggest either just one or two simple frames around the quilt or possibly the same borders as Marianne used on her classic version of the quilt. Why, I ask, are they always in my classes?

QUILTING

Jenny Spencer rose to the challenge, put on her sun glasses and quilted Marianne's Star Bright quilt on her long-arm machine. The quilting design, like the quilt itself, is wild and wacky!

Small but Satisfying

Even when we have completed a large quilt project and the fabric pile in one stash at least is satisfyingly smaller there are always pieces left over – some small, some very small. It is with these remainders in mind that I have included three smaller projects. The sheep in the meadow floor mat plus carrying bag is a new alternative to a cot quilt. By taking it around everywhere in its own bag it will, hopefully, be well-used and equally well-loved. The patchwork pig is ideal for finishing up absolutely everything left at the end of a project. You could even make a matching pig to accompany the quilt – now there's a thought. Do not be daunted by the Japanese patchwork bag: it is not a year's work by hand but is all quick machine work.

Sheep in the Meadow

I designed this fun quilt and matching bag using my favourite blanket stitch appliqué technique. The quilt could be used as a wall-hanging but I have designed it as a floor mat for a baby, with a bag to carry it around in. Hopefully, the bag will encourage the mother to take the quilt around wherever she and the baby go; this way it will become a much-loved comforter rather than an heirloom to be kept pristine and unused. The handles can be dropped down into the bag and the top closed with four spaced squares of Velcro so that it can double as a cushion with the folded quilt inside it.

THE SHEEP STORY

There are lots of sheep in our part of Suffolk, inspiring me to design this rustic quilt to be put on the floor for a baby to lie on. The accompanying bag makes it easier to carry the quilt around. As the baby is likely to treat the quilt with a total lack of respect, it needs to be tough and hard-wearing, so machine-work is more suitable throughout. I did the blanket stitch by hand simply because I'm addicted to doing it this way.

Finished block size 10in x 10in (25.4cm x 25.4cm)
Finished quilt size 40in x 40in (101.6cm x 101.6cm)
Finished bag size 18in x 18in (45.7cm x 45.7cm)

FABRIC REQUIREMENTS FOR QUILT AND BAG

There are two sheep appliqué designs, one front-facing and one side-facing. Another variation can be made by reversing the side-facing pattern to face the other way. Nine sheep are needed for the quilt plus two for the bag, so spend time deciding which of the two designs is going on each of the background fabrics.

◆ Background: 1yd (1m) pale green fabric for four background squares on quilt and one on bag, plus outer quilt border;

2yd (2m) of darker green fabric for five background squares on quilt and one on bag, plus bag lining and handles and quilt binding.

◆ Sheep: ½yd (0.5m) of cream fabric for the bodies;

one fat quarter of another cream fabric for the faces;

one fat quarter of black fabric for eyes and legs plus the black sheep on the bag.

◆ Flowers: 12in (30.5cm) square of orange fabric.

◆ Narrow fence border on quilt: two strips 1½ x 30½in (3.8cm x 77.5cm).

◆ Narrow borders on bag: 12in (30.5cm) of striped fabric.

◆ Quilt wadding and backing: a piece of each 42in x 42in (106.7cm x 106.7cm).

◆ Bag wadding: two squares 20in (50.8cm), plus two strips 2in x 30in (5cm x 76.2cm) for handles.

◆ Thicker thread for blanket stitch appliqué (I used Gütermann silk).

◆ Iron-on fusible web: 2yd (2m) (I used Bondaweb, known in the USA as Wonder-Under).

◆ Velcro (hook-and-loop tape) four 1in (2.5cm) squares for bag top.

Much time is saved in this project by cutting out the sheep and flowers and bonding them on to the background fabric. The raw edges are then blanket stitched by hand or more speedily by machine using a blanket stitch or a zigzag.

These sheep keep appearing in student's pieces – on quilts, on cushions, even on a grand-daughter's pyjamas! The images can be reduced by a photocopier to fit different projects, which opens out the design possibilities even more.

Quilt Construction

This technique uses a fusible web to stick the raw edges of the appliqué pieces on to the background fabric before stitching around the design with blanket stitch. The Bondaweb is used to stick only the outer ⅛in (3mm) of each appliqué piece, to avoid the thick, stiff layers usually associated with fusible work.

MAKING THE SIDE-FACING SHEEP

1 When using fusible web the design must be reversed. Fig 1 (page 114) shows the whole pattern for the side-facing sheep, while Fig 2 (page 114) gives the reversed pattern for cutting the Bondaweb. Trace the shapes in Fig 2 on to the smooth side of the Bondaweb, including any dotted areas, which are areas where one shape is overlapped by another. Mark the numbers and grainline arrows on the tracing, keeping these at the very edge of each shape, as the centre area of Bondaweb will be removed later.

2 Cut out the traced body of the sheep roughly just beyond the outer drawn line (Fig 3). Now carefully cut all around the sheep about ⅛in (3mm) *inside* the drawn outline (Fig 4).

3 Remove the inner piece of Bondaweb and from it cut out roughly the head, legs, eyes and flower shapes.

4 Cut away the Bondaweb about ⅛in (3mm) *inside* the head of the sheep. Do not attempt to cut away the inner areas of the legs, eyes and flower, as they are just too small and fiddly.

Fusible webs are a disaster if they get transferred by a hot iron to the base of the iron or ironing board, spreading nasty black marks. To avoid this, place greaseproof paper on the ironing board before you start and use some between the iron and the fusible web as you stick.

5 Place each cut piece of Bondaweb rough side *down* on the *wrong* side of the chosen fabric, matching the grainline arrow with the grain or weave of the fabric. Press with a hot iron to stick the Bondaweb to the fabric.

6 Now cut accurately along the drawn line through both Bondaweb and fabric. Include any dotted area in the cut-out shape (Fig 5).

Fig 3

cut edge of fusible web

Fig 4

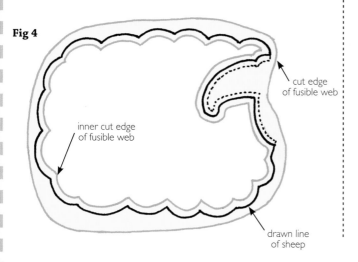

inner cut edge of fusible web

cut edge of fusible web

drawn line of sheep

Fig 5

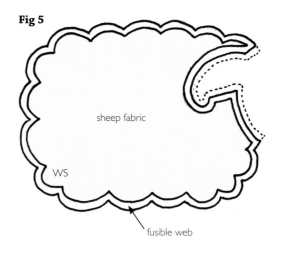

sheep fabric

WS

fusible web

SMALL BUT SATISFYING

7 Remove the paper backing. Arrange the cut shapes on one of the background fabric squares, right side *up*, glue side *down*, using Fig 1 as a guide for positioning each piece. Do not iron anything down until you have arranged all the pieces. Don't try too hard to copy the picture in Fig 1 as slightly different eye positions and legs on each sheep will give them individuality. Start with piece 1 and work in order up to piece 8. Dotted areas need to be overlapped by other pieces. When you are happy with the arrangement, press everything with a hot iron to fix the pieces in place.

> To reverse the direction the sheep are facing, trace Fig 2 and turn it over. Fix the tracing paper on to a sheet of white paper with a couple of paper-clips for easier viewing of the drawn lines before using it as a pattern for cutting out the Bondaweb pieces.

8 Now repeat the process described in steps 1–7 with all the side-facing sheep.

MAKING THE FRONT-FACING SHEEP

9 Fig 6 (page 115) shows the whole, actual size pattern for the front-facing sheep, while Fig 7 (page 116) gives the reversed pattern for cutting the Bondaweb. Follow the instructions for tracing and cutting the Bondaweb given previously for the side-facing sheep. Begin with the two legs when positioning the design (pieces 1 and 2) and finish with the flower (piece 6). Press with a hot iron to fix all the pieces into position.

> This is a perfect project if you are not too experienced with machine quilting and stitching around the edge of appliquéd shapes. The floor quilt is not too big to move around while quilting with the machine, and with any luck the baby will not yet be a discerning quilter so the standard of workmanship need not be an issue.

STITCHING THE DESIGN BY MACHINE

Many modern machines include a blanket stitch in their selection of decorative stitches and this works well around the sheep. Set up a practice piece and try stitching around it to sort out strategies for getting around corners and negotiating curves. Machines vary in their stitches so you need to get out the manual (oh, that old thing. . .) and follow the instructions given for using the stitch patterns. My machine has several features that I find invaluable for blanket stitching, including the needle-down function and the knee-lift, so if you have these, try using them while doing your practice pieces. If preferred, use a simple zigzag to stitch around the designs.

> As a practice piece first draw several leaf shapes on a double thickness of fabric. Stitch around these to get used to stitching curves and going round sharp corners. Then stick some cut leaves on to a background with Bondaweb and get comfortable with stitching around them before trying out the actual design. The stitch is a pain to unpick, so get it right before you start the project.

STITCHING THE DESIGN BY HAND

If you prefer to hand stitch the design, use a slightly thicker thread than usual (I like Gütermann silk thread) and a fine sewing needle such as a sharps 9 or 10. Black is often used to outline this type of design, but any colour will be fine. When blanket stitching around the sheep, try to keep the stitches all the same length, about $3/16$in (5mm) and evenly spaced (Fig 8). When turning sharp corners like the ends of the sheep's ears, make one extra tiny stitch on the spot at the corner to keep that long corner stitch in place (Fig 9).

Fig 8

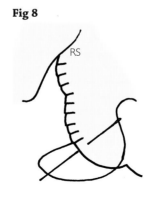

Fig 9

General stitching guidelines

For the side-facing sheep, stitch the edges of the design either by hand or by machine, using a blanket stitch. Stitch around the legs, body and head. Before stitching around the eyes, the layers of the appliqué may be reduced by turning the whole piece over and cutting away the background areas within the blanket-stitched edges ¼in (6mm) away from the stitching. This is not obligatory, so if your nerve fails you just leave the layers intact. I like to cut away the back layers to make quilting easier and to give the quilt more life. Stitch around the edges of each flower with blanket stitch. Stitch the centres of the flowers with the same thread as for the blanket stitching as in Fig 10. Use embroidery thread to hand stitch the flower stems.

Fig 10

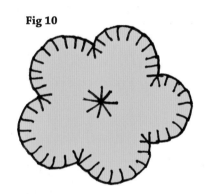

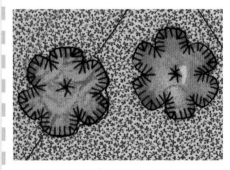

For the front-facing sheep, stitch around the legs and body. Cut away the background fabric behind the body before stitching around the head. Cut away the fabric behind the head before stitching around the eyes. Stitch the flower as for the side-facing sheep.

ASSEMBLING THE QUILT

1 Arrange the completed nine squares as in Fig 11. Stitch together the top row of three squares. Press the seams to one side, ironing from the front of the work. Stitch together the second row of three squares and press the seams in the opposite direction to row 1. Stitch together the third row. Press the seams in the same direction as row 1 (Fig 12).

Fig 11

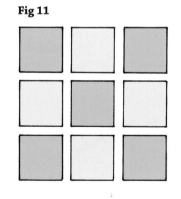

Fig 12

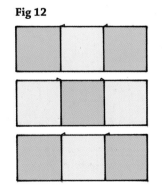

2 Stitch the three rows together to make the centre of the quilt (Fig 13). Press the seams to one side, ironing from the front of the work.

Fig 13

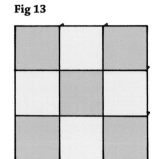

Adding the borders

3 For the first narrow 'fence' border cut two strips each 1½in x 30½in (3.8cm x 77.5cm). Pin and stitch a strip to either side of the quilt. Press the seams outwards, away from the quilt (Fig 14), ironing from the front.

Fig 14

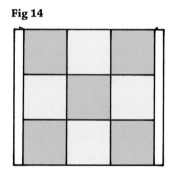

4 Cut two strips of the same fabric, each measuring 1½in x 32½in (3.8cm x 82.6cm). Pin and stitch these to the top and bottom of the quilt. Press the seams outwards, away from the quilt (Fig 15).

Fig 15

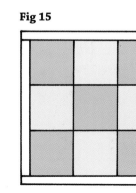

5 For the outer border cut two strips of green fabric each 4in x 32½in (10.2cm x 82.6cm). Pin and stitch these to the sides of the quilt. Press seams outwards (Fig 16).

Fig 16

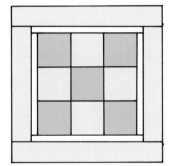

6 Cut two strips of the same green fabric, each measuring 4in x 39½in (10.2cm x 100.3cm). Pin and stitch these to the top and bottom of the quilt. Press the seams outwards (Fig 17).

Fig 17

7 Use Bondaweb to make as many flowers as you wish in the two sizes in Fig 18. Arrange them on the wider border. Don't iron any into position until you are happy with the whole effect. Blanket stitch around each flower and stitch each centre as before.

Fig 18 (actual size)

QUILTING

1 Place the backing fabric, wadding (batting) and quilt top in a layer and pin or tack (baste) the layers together ready for quilting either by hand or machine.

2 Quilt around the sheep, fairly close to the blanket stitching. Leave the sheep themselves unquilted to keep puffy. Quilt along each of the seams between each sheep block – I used a herringbone stitch on my sewing machine with a walking foot to add some interest to the straight seams. I quilted in the ditch on each border strip and added more surface quilting in the final wide border. Either hand or machine quilting is fine, and so is a combination of both. Just do as much or as little as you think is effective (see Ideas for Quilting page 131).

3 Trim the wadding and backing to ¼in (6mm) beyond the quilt top. Finally, bind the edges with green fabric (see Binding a Quilt page 133).

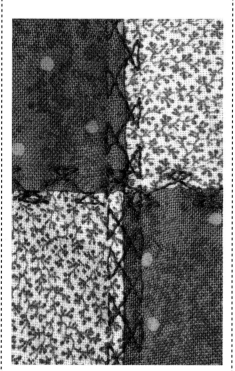

Herringbone stitch was worked by machine along the seams of the blocks.

A personal touch

While I was making this quilt several of my students insisted it needed a sheepdog. This was not part of my overall design but as an afterthought when it was finished I appliquéd a sheepdog on a piece of black fabric, trimmed it down to a ¼in (6mm) beyond the appliqué and then hand-appliquéd the dog to the back of the quilt, turning the edge of background fabric under as I stitched and taking care not to stitch through to the quilt front. This was a one-off that I couldn't give as a pattern as it just evolved, but do consider adding your own personal message on the back of a quilt – perhaps a little in-joke for the person the quilt is for, or your own favourite flower or animal – something as a bonus when you turn the quilt over. Do all the work on a foundation of background fabric and then appliqué it by hand to the quilt back, stitching into the wadding but not through to the front.

The sheepdog on the back of my quilt is a nice personal touch.

Bag Construction

1 Make two more sheep blocks, following the instructions in steps 1–7 on page 108 and using a different background fabric in each block. I made both my blocks with the side-facing sheep, including one black sheep.

2 From the fabric for the narrow borders cut four strips each 1½in x 10½in (3.8cm x 26.7cm) and four strips 1½in x 12½in (3.8cm x 31.8cm).

3 Pin and stitch a shorter strip to either side of each sheep block. Press the seams outwards, away from the block, ironing from the front of the work (Fig 19).

Fig 19

4 Pin and stitch a longer strip to both top and bottom of each block. Press the seams outwards, away from the block as before (Fig 20).

Fig 20

5 From each of the two green background fabrics cut four strips, two 2½in x 12½in (6.4cm x 31.8cm) and two 2½in x 16½in (6.4cm x 42cm). Use the darker green as a border around the lighter sheep background and reverse this for the other block.

6 Pin and stitch a shorter strip to either side of each block. Press the seams outwards.

7 Pin and stitch a longer strip to the top and bottom of each block. Press the seams outwards (Fig 21).

Fig 21

8 From the fabric chosen for the narrow borders cut four strips, two 1½in x 16½in (3.8cm x 42cm) and two 1½in x 18½in (3.8cm x 47cm).

9 Pin and stitch the strips around each block in the same way as the previous borders (Fig 22).

Fig 22

10 Trim both blocks if necessary to exactly 18½in (47cm). If one block is smaller than this measurement, trim both blocks to the smaller measurement.

11 Cut two pieces of wadding (batting) to exactly 18½in x 18½in (47cm x 47cm) or the size of the trimmed blocks if this is different from 18½in (47cm).

12 From the darker green background fabric cut two pieces each measuring 18½in x 19½in (47cm x 49.5cm). Cut each piece into two halves as shown in Fig 23.

Fig 23

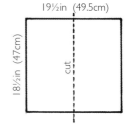

19½in (49.5cm)

18½in (47cm)

cut

13 Stitch each pair of pieces together once more with a ½in (1.2cm) seam, leaving an unstitched section in the centre about 6in (15.2cm) long. Press the seam open, including the unstitched section (Fig 24).

Fig 24

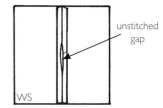

unstitched gap

WS

14 Place a cut square of wadding on a flat surface and position one of the sheep blocks on it, right side *up*. Place a joined piece of backing fabric right side *down* on to it, matching the outer edges of the block and the backing carefully. Pin and stitch a ¼in (6mm) seam round all four sides of the block (Fig 25).

Fig 25

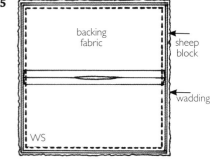

backing fabric

sheep block

wadding

WS

15 Trim the corners of the block to reduce the bulk. Turn the block right side out through the unstitched gap in the seam of the backing fabric. Push the corners out carefully without damaging the stitching. Stitch the gap in the seam of the backing fabric using ladder stitch (page 121).

16 Repeat this process with the second block. You now have two separate finished squares, which will be stitched together to make the bag. Quilt each piece at this stage *before* joining them together.

> **Do all the quilting while the bag is still in two pieces, as once they are stitched together it is very difficult to add any extra quilting or embellishments.**

QUILTING THE BAG

I quilted each block by machine in the same way as the main quilt, also quilting with a machine herringbone stitch along each border seam.

ASSEMBLING THE BAG

1 With right sides facing *outwards*, match the two sides of the bag carefully, especially at the corners. Pin together along the three sides, leaving the top edges open. Stitch the two pieces together by topstitching through all the layers, stitching ¼in (6mm) away from the edges of the bag.

> **To reinforce the seam joining the two parts of the bag together I used a triple-stitch on my machine plus the walking foot. If your machine doesn't have this stitch, stitch around the bag sides twice to give a double strength.**

Making the handles

2 Cut four strips of darker green background fabric each 2in x 30in (5cm x 76.2cm). Also cut two strips of wadding (batting) to the same measurements.

3 Place two fabric strips together with right sides facing. Lay a strip of wadding on top and pin the three layers together. Machine a ¼in (6mm) seam along each of the long two sides (Fig 26). Repeat this with the other two strips of fabric and the wadding strip.

Fig 26

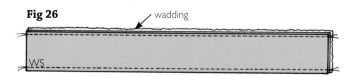

wadding

WS

4 Turn each handle through to the right side and press firmly. Topstitch along each of the two long sides (Fig 27).

Fig 27

RS

5 Trim each end evenly. Fold a ½in (1.2cm) turning and pin or tack (baste) in place (Fig 28).

Fig 28

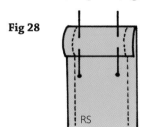

RS

6 Pin each handle to the inside of the bag with the folded turning 2in (5cm) below the top edge of the bag. On the outside of the bag, stitch several times across the handle to secure it, stitching along the seam of the top border so that the stitching is unnoticeable (Fig 29).

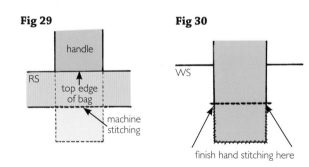

Fig 29

handle

RS

top edge of bag

machine stitching

Fig 30

WS

finish hand stitching here

7 On the inside of the bag, hand stitch the handle ends firmly to the bag. Leave the top inch of strap above the machine stitching unstitched (Fig 30) as this makes it easier to drop the handles down into the bag when you want to convert it into a cushion.

Adding the Velcro

8 To finish your bag, take the four 1in x 1in (2.5cm x 2.5cm) squares of Velcro and separate the two layers. Pin the four soft pieces to the inside top edge of one side of the bag, spacing them evenly along its length. Stitch them firmly by hand, trying not to take the stitches through to the front of the bag. Repeat this with the four scratchy pieces of Velcro on the other side of the bag, positioning them so that they exactly match the soft Velcro and will stick together when the top edges of the bag are closed.

Fig 1 (actual size)

Fig 2 (actual size)

Fig 6 (actual size)

Fig 7 (actual size)

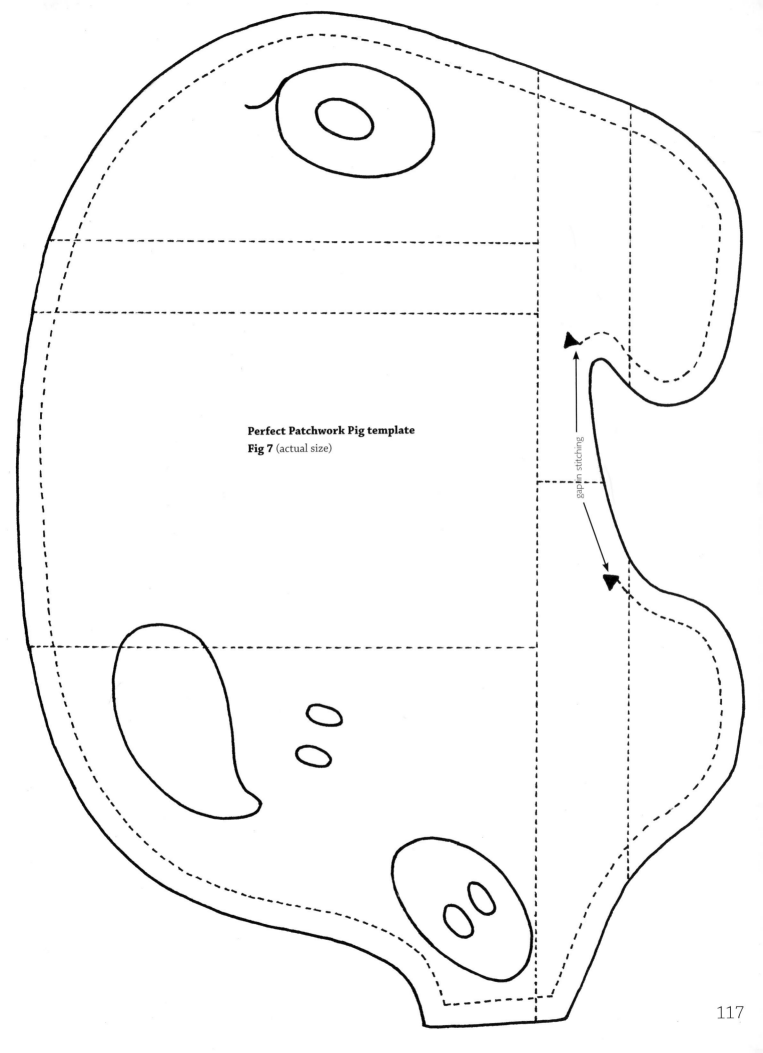

Perfect Patchwork Pig template
Fig 7 (actual size)

gaplin stitching

Perfect Patchwork Pig

This patchwork pig is perfect in several ways: he is astonishingly quick and easy to make, is the perfect size to tuck under a small arm at bed-time, or even a bigger arm ... plus the fabric required really is just a few scraps and leftovers. I've stitched two versions, both in pretty pastels, shown opposite with the original pig.

THE PIG STORY

Some years ago when I was at a huge quilt show in Houston, Texas, I spotted a patchwork soft toy pig on a stall selling antique quilts and fabrics. The pig was old and decidedly faded and worn but I just had to buy him. I knew that my friend Wendy would love him too, so he would be her Christmas present. Part of the pig's appeal was the way his face was embroidered all on one side – anatomically incorrect but charming. I also liked the use of the many fabrics to make the patchwork out of which the pig shape had been cut. I decided to draft a pattern to make a pig for myself: this would give me a reason to break into one of those irresistible little parcels of assorted fabrics tied up with ribbon, which I had bought ostensibly to use but really just to admire as a collector's item.

Finished size 9½in x 7½in (24cm x 19cm)

FABRIC REQUIREMENTS

◆ The pig is cut from two pieces of patchwork, each measuring 11½in x 8¾in (29.2cm x 22.2cm). The layout of the patchwork pieces for the back of the pig has to be a mirror image of the front, otherwise the two halves do not match.

◆ Seven fabrics are used for the patchwork (A–G) – if there isn't enough of one fabric just substitute another or use it for one of the smaller shapes in the patchwork. I used the same fabrics for both the front and back of the pig, but you can use a different set of fabrics for the back if you wish.

◆ Embroidery thread in a contrasting colour.

◆ Polyester stuffing.

The complex piecing of each side of the patchwork pig is done at the start of the project when it is really quick and simple to do. Rectangles of different fabrics are stitched together to make two larger pieces from which the two pig outlines are then cut.

Construction

PIECING THE PATCHWORK

1 Choose seven fabrics to make into the two patchwork blocks, one block for the front of the pig (Fig 1) and one for the back (Fig 2). Fig 3 shows the sizes of the pieces of fabric to be cut. Remember that fabric A will be the face of the pig and fabric D his rear end. Assuming that the same fabrics are to be used for both front and back of the pig, cut the following pieces:

Fabric A – cut two of rectangle A each 6½in x 4¾in (16.5cm x 12cm);

Fabric B – cut two of rectangle B each 6½in x 4in (16.5cm x 10.1cm);

Fabric C – cut two of rectangle C each 6½in x 1¼in (16.5cm x 3.2cm);

Fabric D – cut two of rectangle D each 6½in x 3in (16.5cm x 7.6cm);

Fabric E – cut two of rectangle E each 6½in x 1½in (16.5cm x 3.8cm);

Fabric F – cut two of rectangle F each 5½in x 1½in (14cm x 3.8cm);

Fabric G – cut two of rectangle G each 11½in x 1¾in (29.2cm x 4.4cm).

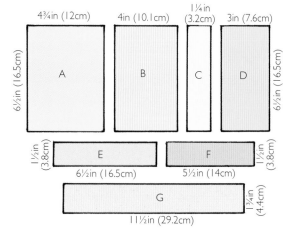

Fig 3

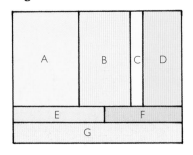

Fig 1 – front

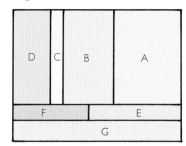

Fig 2 – back

2 Following the plan shown in Fig 1, stitch together one of each of A, B, C and D to form a strip (Fig 4), using ¼in (6mm) seams throughout. Press the seams to one side, ironing from the front of the work.

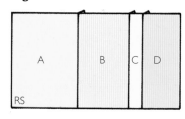

Fig 4

3 Join one each of E and F together to make one long strip (Fig 5). Press the seam to one side as before.

Fig 5

4 Stitch this to the bottom of the block (Fig 6). Press the long seam towards pieces E and F.

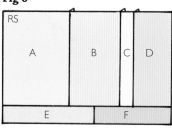

Fig 6

5 Finally, add strip G. This completes the block for the *front* of the pig as seen in Fig 1.

6 To make the block for the *back* of the pig, arrange the cut rectangles A, B, C, D, E, F and G as shown in Fig 2. Join the pieces together row by row in the same way as for the block for the front of the pig. You should finish up with one block with the pieces arranged as in Fig 1 and the other block as in Fig 2.

SMALL BUT SATISFYING

MAKING UP THE PIG

1 Make a pattern for the pig by tracing Fig 7 on page 117 on to tracing paper and cutting it out. Include all the dotted lines in the tracing plus the two triangles to show the gap in the stitching.

2 Pin the paper pattern on to the *front* of the patchwork block shown in Fig 1 (the front of the pig), matching the seams of the piecing with the dotted lines on the pig pattern. This is not critical, just a guide for positioning, so if your seams do not match perfectly with the pattern it won't matter too much.

3 Cut around the paper pattern exactly to create the front side of the pig. No extra seam allowances are needed.

4 Turn the paper pattern over so that the pig is facing to the *right*. Pin the pattern on to the *front* of the patchwork block shown in Fig 2 (the back of the pig), matching the seams of the piecing with the dotted lines on the pattern as before. Now cut around the paper pattern to create the back of the pig.

5 At this stage transfer the drawn lines of the eyes, ear, nose and tail to the *right* side of the pig's front, either by tracing with a light box or by using dressmaker's transfer paper. All the features are on the front side of the pig, with none on the back.

> **!** If you leave the marking of his face until after you have stitched and stuffed the pig, it will be too late to trace it – you will have to copy it freehand from the original in Fig 7.

6 Stitch the lines by hand with embroidery thread in a contrasting colour, using backstitch or stem stitch (Fig 8).

Fig 8 Stem stitch

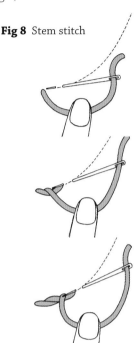

7 Place the front and back sections of the pig together with right sides facing. Pin the layers together. Starting at a marked triangle, stitch a ¼in (6mm) seam around the shape, leaving a gap between the two triangles as indicated on the pattern. Clip any curved edges, making the clips about ¼in (6mm) apart and taking care not to clip right to the stitched line as this would weaken the stitching (Fig 9).

Fig 9

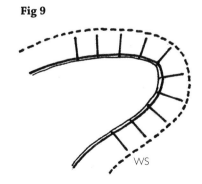

WS

8 Turn the pig to the right side through the gap in the stitching. Fill with stuffing until the pig is comfortably solid. Stitch up the opening using ladder stitch to make the stitching as inconspicuous as possible (Fig 10).

Fig 10 Ladder stitch

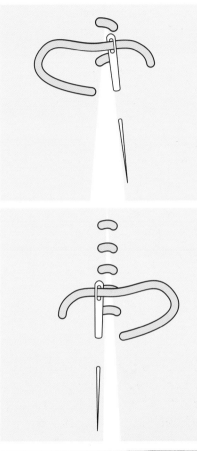

Japanese Folded Patchwork Bag

Some of the students in my classes, from far-flung Hatfield Peverel in Essex, were involved in a local challenge for making a bag using the Japanese folded patchwork technique. They kindly passed on the instructions to me, but as soon as I saw that I had to start by gathering twenty-eight circles of fabric with tiny running stitches around circles of card I began to lose the will to live. So I worked out an alternative, much faster method using the machine. Too late for the Hatfield Peverel girls, who toiled for weeks over their exquisite bags, but here it is for the rest of us fashion victims who need the bag sooner rather than later.

THE BAG STORY

When I was working out a quicker method I first made the black and white version, using red fabric as the lining, which shows just as a sliver around each curved edge. I was determined to use the sewing machine throughout, so the curved edges of the classic block (Fig 1) were all top-stitched in place with toning black thread. I made the handles shorter than in the general instructions and the result is a snappy little number quite worthy of a fashion magazine. The second bag (below) was made from my favourite mauve-pink batiks and has longer handles. I constructed the blocks, machine stitched them together, then stitched the squares into place by hand while travelling in the United States. Because of the hand stitching this bag has a softer, more ethnic look than the black and white version.

Finished block size 3½in x 3½in (8.9cm x 8.9cm)
Finished bag size (without handles) 14in x 10½in (35.6cm x 26.7cm)

FABRIC REQUIREMENTS

◆ 24in (61cm) of the main fabric for the bag.

◆ 24in (61cm) of a second fabric to line each circle. This only shows at the very edge of each folded circle, so choose a fabric that blends with the main fabric. It is only there to make the stitching process easier and is therefore wasted, so now is the time to use up fabric you really would like to get rid of.

◆ ½yd (0.5m) of fabric for the centres of each folded circle and for the bag handles.

◆ Twenty-eight squares of thin wadding each 3¼in x 3¼in (8.3cm x 8.3cm), plus two strips each 2in x 20in (5cm x 50.8cm).

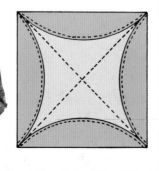

Fig 1

Japanese folded patchwork is usually stitched by hand, gathering fabric circles around card and hand stitching the folded units to each other. For a fashion item like a bag a less tortuous and quicker machine technique makes more sense, especially as machined seams make the bag stronger. The curved edges may be stitched down by machine or hand.

SMALL BUT SATISFYING

Construction

MAKING THE FOLDED PATCHWORK UNITS

1 From both the main bag fabric and the lining fabric cut four strips 5¾in (14.6cm) wide. Place a strip of each fabric together with right sides facing.

2 Make a template from the circle in Fig 2 by tracing it, cutting it out and sticking it on to card, or use template plastic. If you have a set of circles for rotary cutting use the 5½in (14cm) circle. This is a machined technique, so the seam allowance is included in the template.

3 Draw round the circle template on the layered strips of fabric twenty-eight times (Fig 3). Pin each drawn circle in the centre through both layers of fabric before cutting out each circle on the drawn line. If you are using a rotary cutting circle just place the circle on the layered strips and cut around it using a small rotary cutter.

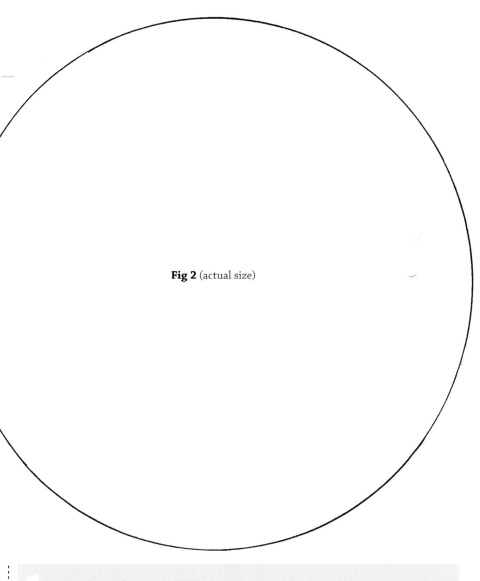

Fig 2 (actual size)

> **!** Do not separate the two layers of circles after they have been cut: cutting them from layered strips means that the grain or weave of both fabrics have been matched and once separated it is hard to match up the grain on the two circles again.

Fig 3

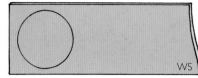

WS

4 Machine stitch a ¼in (6mm) seam around each pair of circles (Fig 4).

5 Trim the seam allowance down to about ⅛in (3mm) – if you have a pair of pinking shears, use these to reduce the bulk of the seam allowance (Fig 5).

6 Carefully cut a slit about 2½in (6.4cm) long in the lining fabric of each circle. Do not cut through to the main fabric! Keep the slit in the centre of the shape, following the grainline or weave of the fabric (Fig 6).

Fig 4

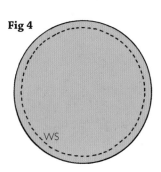

WS

Fig 5

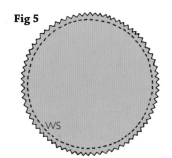

WS

Fig 6

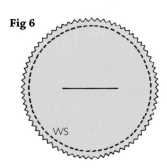

WS

7 Turn each circle right side out through the cut slit. Run a hera (see below) or a similar tool inside the circle along the seam to push the edges of the fabric out to make a true circle (Fig 7). Press well. Make twenty-eight of these turned circles and press each with an iron.

Fig 7

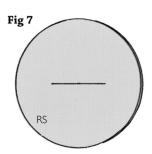

RS

I use a hera for all sorts of quilting tasks, especially marking fabric for quilting. Used for straight lines against the side of a ruler it marks the fabric by compacting the fibres, which shows up as a line on the fabric. To remove a line, just dampen the fabric and allow it to dry naturally. The fibres of the fabric swell as they dry and the line disappears.

Marking the circles

8 Cut a square from template plastic measuring 3½in x 3½in (8.9cm x 8.9cm). Place the plastic square on to the lining side of one of the fabric circles, keeping the grain of the fabric and the cut slit parallel with the top and bottom of the plastic square (Fig 8). Draw round the plastic square using a fine marking pencil. Repeat this on the lining side of each of the twenty-eight circles.

Fig 8

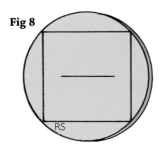

RS

You may find the plastic square slightly too large to fit on to the fabric circle with all its corners just touching the edge of the circle. If so, don't worry, just trim the plastic square down slightly until it fits as in Fig 8.

Joining the circles

9 Place two circles with right sides together and both slits running across each circle as in Fig 9.

Fig 9

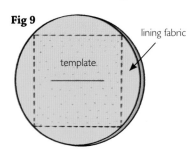

lining fabric

template

10 Pin and stitch the two side drawn lines marked AB in Fig 10, matching the edges of the circles exactly. Open out the circles and press back the two stitched edges firmly with an iron (Fig 11).

Fig 10

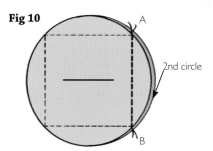

A

2nd circle

B

Fig 11

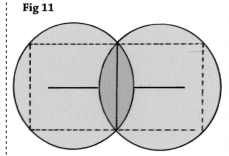

11 Use the same method to pin and stitch together a row of eight circles (Fig 12). Press firmly.

Fig 12

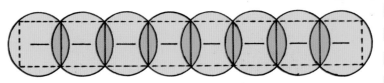

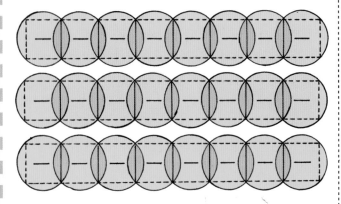

12 Pin and stitch two more rows of eight circles, making a total of three rows (Fig 13).

Fig 13

13 Carefully pin and stitch the top two rows together, matching the drawn horizontal lines on each circle and the outer edges of the circles. Press back the stitched edges firmly (Fig 14).

Fig 14

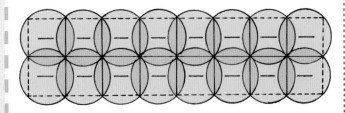

14 Pin and stitch row 3 to row 2 in the same way. Press the stitched edges back as before (Fig 15).

Fig 15

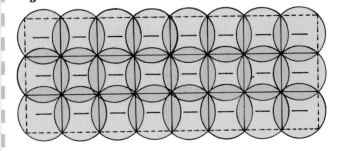

15 Now join the remaining four circles into pairs as shown in Fig 16.

Fig 16

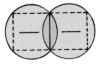

16 Add these to the bottom row of circles (Fig 17). These four extra circles will eventually form the bag base.

Fig 17

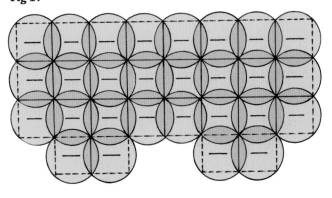

What you should now have is the entire bag minus handles joined together as one flat piece. It is so much easier to add all the centres at this stage, joining the sides and bottom to make the bag shape afterwards.

Adding the centres

17 From the fabric chosen for the centres of the circles cut twenty-eight squares each 3½in x 3½in (8.9cm x 8.9cm). From the wadding (I used Hobbs Heirloom 80/20) cut twenty-eight squares each 3¼in x 3¼in (8.3cm x 8.3cm).

18 Place a square of wadding in the centre of a drawn square on one stitched circle. It will be slightly smaller than the drawn square. Place a square of centre fabric on top of the wadding, right side upwards. It should overlap the wadding by about ⅛in (3mm) on all sides with its edges matching the drawn square on the circle. If the centre square overlaps the drawn square, trim it to fit exactly. Pin or tack (baste) the centre firmly in place (Fig 18). Repeat this in each of the twenty-eight stitched circles.

Fig 18

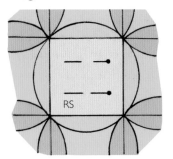

RS

SMALL BUT SATISFYING

19 Fold the curved edges of each circle over the centre square on all sides. Pin or tack (baste) in position, taking care to cover the raw edges of the centre fabrics at the corners. Leave the curved edges at either end unturned as in Fig 19.

Fig 19

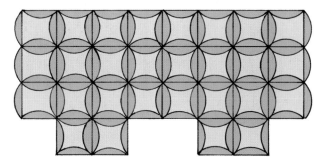

I find that just one pin placed in the centre of each curved side is enough to hold everything in place as you stitch (Fig 20).

Fig 20

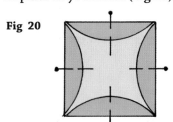

20 Topstitch the curved edges by machine or hand quilt them in place using a large stitch in contrasting thread. More decorative stitching can be done in each centre if you wish.

ASSEMBLING THE BAG

1 Pin and stitch the two end sections together by machine in the usual way, to make a tube, marked as number 1 in Fig 21. Press the curved edges back and stitch them into place on each circle to match the rest of the design.

2 To construct the base, turn the tube inside out. Swing the edges of each pair of base squares round to meet the bottom edge of the adjacent squares, shown as number 2 in Fig 21. Oversew these edges together firmly by hand.

Fig 21

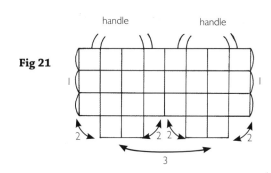

3 Finally, stitch the centre seam of the bag base together (number 3 in Fig 21) by oversewing firmly by hand. Turn the bag right side out.

Making the handles

4 Cut four strips of the fabric used for the circle centres each 2in x 20in (5cm x 50.8cm). Cut two strips of thin wadding to the same measurements. If longer handles are required, cut all strips 2in x 30in (5cm x 76.2cm).

5 Place two fabric strips together with right sides facing. Lay a strip of wadding on top and pin the three layers together. Machine a ¼in (6mm) seam along each of the two long sides (Fig 22). Repeat this with the other two strips of fabric and the wadding strip.

Fig 22

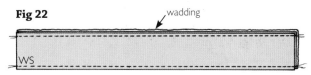

wadding

WS

6 Turn each handle through to the right side and press firmly. Topstitch along each of the two long sides (Fig 23).

Fig 23

RS

7 Trim each end evenly. Fold a ½in (1.2cm) turning and pin or tack (baste) it in place (Fig 24).

Fig 24

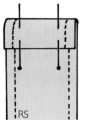

RS

8 Position each strip on the bag as shown in Fig 21 with the folded turning placed against the inside of the bag. Hand stitch the handle ends firmly to the bag to finish.

Finishing a Quilt

Once the main quilt has been completed there begin the decisions on making borders, quilting and binding. All too often there just isn't enough fabric from the quilt left at this stage, but hunt through that stash – the perfect fabric could be lurking there. If not, what a lovely reason for visiting a quilt shop and buying some more. Do not rush this stage of the quilt: well-designed borders and quilting can elevate a pleasing quilt into something quite special.

This final section provides general information on finishing your quilt and includes how to make borders, back your quilt and bind the edges. There are also some ideas on quilting.

BORDERING A QUILT

Hopefully the borders shown on each project quilt will appeal, but there may be a problem with having enough fabric left over to make them. Quilts do not always have to have borders: some quilts look best without any extra border at all, like Heather Jackson's quilt on page 62. Others are so busy that they just need one or two simple frames around them. Both Yvonne Dawson (her Bargello quilt is on page 34) and Julia Reed (her Scrap Lattice quilt is on page 80) framed the main quilt, then added more piecing and finished with a second wider frame. This is a really effective way to extend a quilt when the fabric will only stretch to the size of the top of the bed. The quilt and its inner frame fit nicely on the bed top while the new added-on fabric used in the extra pieced section drops vertically down the sides of the bed. The final wide border around the outer edge of the quilt completes the design.

If your existing quilt fabric will not stretch to this, let the borders wait until you have found a new fabric that will frame the quilt well and use that. It doesn't matter if a fabric has not been used in the quilt as long as it looks as though it belongs. A 3in–4in (7.5cm–10cm) border for a bed quilt can be cut from 1yd (1m) of fabric, while 1½yd (1.37m) would give a wider border with just one central join on each side. You can get away with several joins in a border strip provided they are placed at regular intervals so that they look planned.

Adding framing borders

1 Lay the quilt top on a flat surface and measure its length down the *centre*, not the edge. If you always do this and cut the borders to match the centre measurements there is less danger of the quilt edges spreading to give wavy borders.

2 Cut two strips of border fabric in the chosen width to match the quilt measurement – these will make the side borders. Pin and stitch each side strip to the quilt, easing in any fullness in the quilt as you pin. Work on a flat surface and match the centres and both ends before pinning the rest. Press the seams outwards, away from the quilt (Fig 1).

3 Measure the quilt plus side borders from side to side across the centre. Cut two strips of border fabric in the chosen width to match this measurement. Pin and stitch these to the top and bottom of the quilt, matching centres and both ends (Fig 2). Press the seams outwards from the quilt.

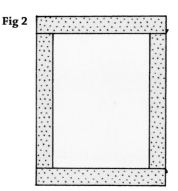

Fig 2

4 If another border is planned, measure the quilt down its centre and repeat the process, sides first and then top and bottom.

5 You may prefer to make your border with cornerstones, that is, a square of different fabric in each corner of the border (Fig 3). Measure the quilt across its centre in *both* directions and cut strips of the border fabric in your chosen width and in lengths to match these measurements. Stitch the side strips to the quilt as usual. Press the seams outwards away from the quilt.

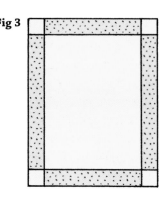

Fig 3

Fig 1

6 Cut four squares of fabric for the cornerstones the same size as the cut width of the border strips. Stitch one of these to either end of both top and bottom border strips (Fig 4).

Fig 4

Press the seams towards the long strip. Pin and stitch these border strips to the top and bottom of the quilt, matching seams carefully (Fig 5). Press seams outwards, away from the quilt.

Fig 5

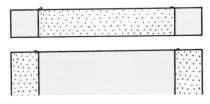

If a second border with cornerstones is planned, re-measure the quilt after the first border is added and repeat the process (Fig 6).

Fig 6

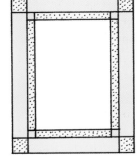

Pieced borders

Having framed your quilt with one fabric, you may decide it needs a pieced border next. One option is to echo an element of the main quilt design in the pieced border. Sheila Piper used leftover black and white strips from her blocks to make the 'piano-keys' border around her quilt on page 67. Yvonne Dawson took strips left from her Bargello quilt (page 34) and joined them end to end into long strips which she stitched in three rows around her quilt to make the middle pieced border.

A pieced border gives the chance to really use up the leftovers, even if they have to be supplemented with extra, new fabrics. As long as the colours tone with the quilt, pieces of fabric scrounged from quilter friends to add to your own will fit in surprisingly well.

Borders that use a specific repeated design like the Seminole border on Marianne Bennett's quilt on page 91 can be a problem, as it is not always possible to make repeat designs for border strips in an exact measurement to fit the quilt. There is a cunning strategy to make this easier. First, the border strips are pieced, making them slightly longer than the sides of the quilt. Then one or more extra framing strips are added all around the quilt to bring it up to the correct size to fit the borders. Marianne did a variation of this. She first added a border to the quilt that was wider than she needed. Then she made the Seminole strips, including the mitred corners, to fit as nearly as possible the outer edges of this border, shorter rather than longer. She then trimmed the border down to fit the pieced strips exactly.

Marianne Bennett's inner border is trimmed so that the Seminole turns the corner nicely.

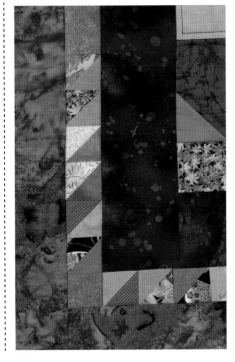

Shirley Prescott played around with the middle border frame on her Tumbling Leaves quilt, using all the leftover triangles from the main quilt to make an unusual pieced border (page 71).

BACKING A QUILT

Finding five or seven yards or metres of fabric for the back of a quilt is another good way of using up your stored yardage. It is quite possible to combine several fabrics in a quilt back which can also create extra interest. If you have a piece of something special that you just cannot bear to cut up, use it as the centre panel of the quilt back and build out from it with strips of other complementary fabrics (Fig 1). Make the piecing as simple as possible since it is more difficult to match exactly the front and back designs if the back is too complex.

Fig 1

A simple series of wide vertical strips in different fabrics can be very pleasing (Fig 2).

Fig 2

If the fabric lengths are not enough for this, add horizontal strips at the top and bottom (Fig 3).

Fig 3

Should you hanker to combine quilt leftovers in an intricate pieced design for the back, limit this to the centre area and surround it with wide strips or pieces of other fabrics (Fig 4). If the back shifts a little during quilting and finishes up not quite square against the front, this is far more noticeable when there are narrow border strips around the edges of the quilt back.

Do not agonize that the quilting done from the front will not relate to the piecing on the back. It is surprising how compatible they seem when you turn the quilt over. Just take extra care when putting the layers together to centre both front and back sections as accurately as possible.

Fig 4

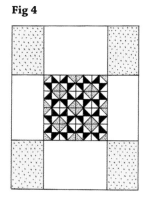

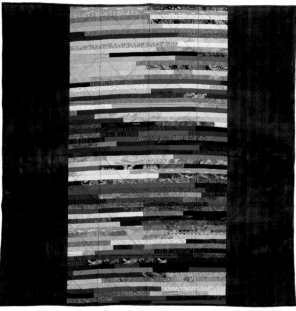

Large pieces of fabric can be used as a pieced backing to a quilt or a collection of smaller strips leftover from the quilt front. If these are limited, then simply add wider strips to each side.

IDEAS FOR QUILTING

When the quilt top is completed and layered with wadding (batting) and backing, the next consideration is how to quilt it. I am not concerned here with the various techniques of quilting – there are plenty of books that deal with this aspect. What I am suggesting is that you find a way of quilting the project that gives you the most satisfaction.

The first question is – do you *like* quilting? Do you enjoy quilting by hand or by machine? If you need to get it done quickly, a simple grid of machine quilting might be best. If you crave hand-work that is always there to be picked up at odd moments it is worth the laborious tacking (basting) of the quilt layers ready for weeks or even months of satisfying activity.

Consider the person for whom the quilt is being made: are they worth months of hand quilting? Do they need an heirloom or will they then be too intimidated to use the quilt at all? I am not being unkind or judgemental, just realistic!

If you feel you need more practice at quilting, especially machine quilting, a small quilt made for someone who will love using it but knows nothing about sewing is the perfect project. Just restrain yourself from pointing out all the faults when they admire it: they will never notice unless you insist on showing them.

Remember that you are allowed to combine hand and machine quilting. I find tacking (basting) a large quilt very tedious and do not have the space to do it efficiently at home, so will often safety pin the layers thoroughly and begin with a skeleton design of machine quilting using a walking foot to keep everything in place. Then I will add more intricate quilting by hand, removing the safety pins where necessary to accommodate my quilting hoop. Some day soon I am going to start filling up areas with free-machine quilting, using some of those wonderful variegated threads that look so exciting. These first efforts will definitely be used on projects for non-critical small children so I can improve my techniques while still making real quilts, not just practice pieces.

I am also encouraging my students to explore the embroidery stitches that so many of us have on our machines. It is surprisingly easy to combine one of these with the walking foot to create a line of decorative stitching through all the layers to act as quilting. Choose a simple pattern like a herringbone, avoiding any that make a design with satin stitch as these can get stuck at seam junctions and build up into a lump. Always make a little sample of a top layer, wadding and backing to experiment with before starting on the quilt – decorative stitches take forever to unpick so make all the mistakes and adjustments on the practice piece. You may find that the width or length of the stitches can be altered. Reducing the stitch width can make a pattern less dominant while increasing the stitch length can stretch the pattern out and make it easier to use as quilting.

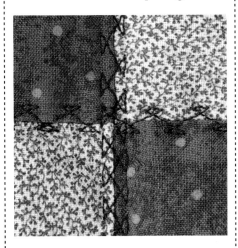

Many sewing machines have a range of useful decorative stitches that can become part of the quilting. I used herringbone on my sheep quilt.

Free-machine quilting, when the underneath feed-dogs are dropped and you just doodle with the needle going in any direction that takes your fancy, needs lots of committed practice before you are good enough to try it on a real quilt. Julia Reed's Batik Lattice quilt on page 81 is free-machine quilted throughout. Her technique is brilliant and she gets better every day because she just loves doing it and cannot leave it alone. That's the trick of course – keeping at it. That's also why I will never excel at it, because I enjoy quilting by hand and with the walking foot too much. Still, I can dream . . .

Detail of the flowers, leaves and swirls machine quilted on the Batik Lattice quilt.

You might feel that some projects will look better without any obvious quilting and prefer to tie the layers together. I have given detailed instructions for this technique overleaf as it is not always covered in general quilting books.

If you really do not enjoy quilting at all or just do not have the time, there is always the option of getting the quilt professionally quilted with a long-arm machine. My Squares on Point quilt on page 51 was quilted in this way by Jenny Spencer from Mildenhall in Suffolk and Jean Campbell had her Tilted Log Cabin quilt (page 27) quilted by Jan Chandler, both experts in their craft. Both of us were really pleased with the finished designs and enjoyed seeing someone else's ideas used on our quilts. I feel no guilt about not doing everything myself. I love quilting but like most quilters have too many ideas and not enough time to make them all. If you want to use someone else's talents to complete a project, find a professional quilter whose work you admire and enjoy her expertise.

Enjoyment is definitely the word here. If quilting is not a pleasure for you, explore the alternatives and keep the dutiful aspects to a minimum. If, like me, you love it, have one quilting project constantly available so that it is always there to soothe and give solace (the hand quilting) or to excite and stimulate (the machine quilting).

Detail of the long-arm quilting, pretty stars and swirls, on my Squares on Point quilt.

Knotting or tying a quilt

Tying the layers of a quilt together with small knots is an efficient way of holding everything in place, either instead of quilting or alongside the quilting in areas like seam junctions where an extra holding-down action is needed. I have always made a double reef knot (thanks to my Girl Guide training) but recently have discovered a slip knot used apparently in Amish quilts which is quick, easy and secure.

1 Mark the position of each knot to be made with a glass-headed pin. If you remove the pins one by one as you make each knot you will know which ones still need to be processed. Knots can be made either on the front of the quilt as part of the design or on the back. For really discreet knotting, work from the back of the quilt using thread that matches the front, changing the thread colour where necessary. The small bar stitch on the quilt front will be scarcely noticeable. Knots need to be a maximum of 3in–4in (7.5cm–10cm) apart if they are the only method of holding the layers of the quilt together.

2 To make a knot, use a double thickness of normal sewing thread or thicker embroidery thread if you prefer. Quilting thread is not suitable as it is waxed and is too springy to hold the knot securely. Working from whichever side of the quilt that the knots will be made, push the needle straight through all the quilt layers. Pull the needle through, leaving about 2in (5cm) of thread on the surface of the quilt. Bring the needle straight back up through the quilt about ⅛in–¼in (3mm–6mm) away from the point where it came through (Fig 1).

3 Hold the 2in (5cm) length of thread straight. Take the needle behind it to the left, then across the front to the right (Fig 2). Bring the needle up through the loop to form a slip knot

(Fig 3). Now pull the needle until the knot begins to tighten (Fig 4).

4 Finally, pull both ends of the thread to tighten the knot. Trim both threads to about ⅜in (5mm) or leave them longer if you want a more decorative effect.

Fig 1

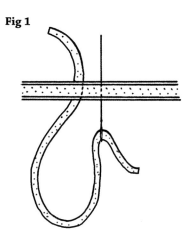

Fig 2

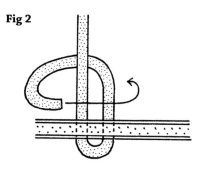

Fig 3

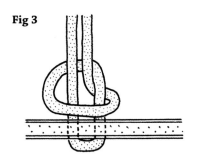

Fig 4

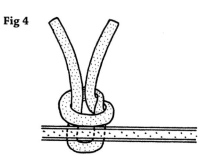

BINDING A QUILT

I have given two methods for binding a quilt; one that uses four strips of binding with squared corners, which is suitable for designs with a horizontal and vertical emphasis such as sashed quilts, and one that uses continuous binding with mitred corners.

Before adding the final binding, check that the quilt lies flat and that the corners are really square. Tacking or basting with small stitches near to the edge of the quilt will help keep the quilt flat and avoid wavy edges. Trim the wadding (batting) and backing fabric down to a scant ¼in (6mm) beyond the quilt top (Fig 1).

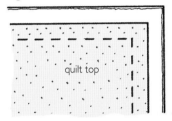

Fig 1

quilt top

It is quite likely that the strips for the binding will have to be joined to make the lengths needed for the quilt. You may even want to add to the overall design with a multi-fabric binding where many short lengths have been joined. The binding will lie flatter and be easier to handle if the joins are made on the bias, making a 45-degree angle with the long edges of the strip. When stitching the binding to the quilt, use a walking foot on your machine so that all the layers are fed through the machine evenly.

Joining the strips

1 Cut all strips for the binding 2½in (6.3cm) wide. Trim the ends of each strip at an angle of 45 degrees as in Fig 2. To do this, position the 45 degrees on a rotary ruler along the top of the strip and cut along the ruler's edge (Fig 3).

Fig 2

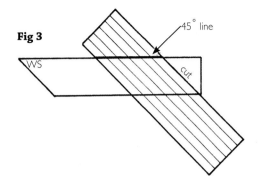

Fig 3

2 To join the strips, place two strips as in Fig 4 with right sides facing. Stitch a ¼in (6mm) seam as shown. Press the diagonal seam open.

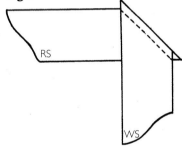

Fig 4

Square-cornered binding

1 Cut four strips of fabric for the binding, each 2½in (6.3cm) wide. The two side strips should measure the length of the quilt from top to bottom. The two strips for the top and bottom edges should measure the width of the quilt from side to side plus 1½in (3.8cm). Shorter lengths can be joined if you do not have enough fabric.

2 Take each side binding strip and fold it in half, right side *outwards*, without pressing. Pin a folded strip to one side of the quilt, matching the edges of the binding with the edge of the quilt top (Fig 5). Stitch a seam ¼in (6mm) from the edge of the quilt top

through all the layers (Fig 6). Repeat this with the 2nd strip on the other side of the quilt.

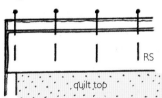

Fig 5

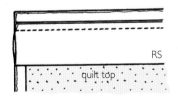

Fig 6

3 Now bring the folded edge of the binding over to the back of the quilt and stitch by hand, just covering the line of machine stitches (Fig 7).

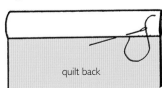

Fig 7

quilt back

4 Pin and stitch the folded binding to the top and bottom of the quilt in the same way, leaving about ¾in (1.9cm) of binding extending beyond the quilt at each end (Fig 8). Trim this back to about ½in (1.2cm) and fold in over the quilt edge (Fig 9).

Fig 8

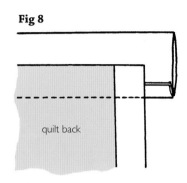

quilt back

Fig 9

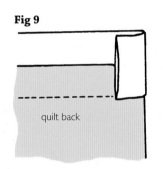

quilt back

Finally, fold the binding over to the back of the quilt and slipstitch in place (Fig 10). Make sure that the corners are really square before you stitch them.

Fig 10

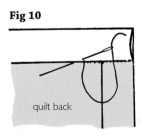

quilt back

Continuous binding with mitred corners

1 Make a length of binding strip 2½in (6.3cm) wide and long enough to go right round the quilt, plus about 11in (28cm) to allow for turning corners and overlapping at start and finish. Both ends of the binding should be trimmed on the diagonal as in Fig 2 (page 133).

2 Fold the binding in half lengthwise, right side outwards, and press the entire length. Fold and press a ¼in (6mm) seam to the wrong side of one diagonal end of the length of binding (Fig 11).

Fig 11

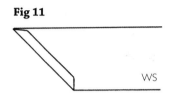

WS

3 Starting with this folded end, pin the folded binding strip along one side of the quilt, matching the edges of the binding with the edge of the quilt top. Do not begin at a corner of the quilt. Instead, make the start and finish of the binding some way down one side where it will be less obvious (Fig 12). Pin to exactly ¼in (6mm) from the nearest corner of the quilt top. Mark this point on the binding with a dot (Fig 13).

Fig 12

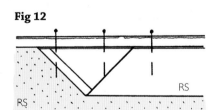

RS

RS

Fig 13

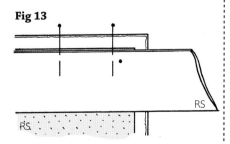

RS

RS

4 Begin stitching 4in–5in (10–12.5cm) from the start of the pinned binding, using a ¼in (6mm) seam allowance. Finish exactly on the marked dot, backstitching to secure the seam.

5 Remove the quilt from the machine and place it on a flat surface ready for pinning the next side. Fold the binding back at right angles from the stitched side (Fig 14).

Fig 14

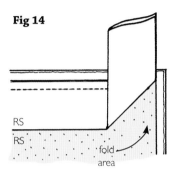

RS

RS

fold area

6 Fold the binding down again with the top fold level with the edge of the wadding and backing and the raw edges level with the edge of the quilt top (Fig 15).

Fig 15

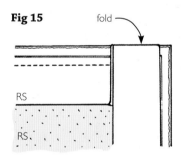

fold

RS

RS

7 Pin the folded layers in place and continue to pin the binding to the side of the quilt until it reaches the next corner. Mark the turning corner ¼in (6mm) from the edge of the quilt top with a dot as before.

8 Stitch the pinned binding with the usual ¼in (6mm) seam, starting at the edge of the quilt (Fig 16) and continuing to the marked dot. Backstitch to secure seam at the dot.

Fig 16

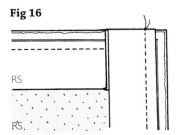

9 Continue to pin and stitch the binding to the quilt, one side at a time, using the method above for turning each corner. On the final side where the binding starts and finishes, slip the finishing end of the strip

between the layers of the other end of the binding. Trim it so that the folded edge of the beginning section overlaps the end piece by about ½in (1.2cm) (Fig 17). Pin the overlapping sections and stitch.

Fig 17

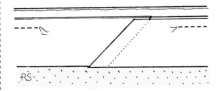

10 Fold the binding over to the back of the quilt and stitch it by hand in the same way as the square-cornered binding. The front corners will form a neat mitre, which can be tweaked into place and left unstitched

as a diagonal fold (Fig 18). The diagonal overlap where the two ends of binding meet can be left unstitched, or made more secure by hand stitching in a matching thread. The corners on the back of the quilt should be arranged into a mitre by folding one side down and then the other side. Arrange the fold in the opposite direction to the fold on the front to distribute the layers evenly and make a flat corner.

Fig 18

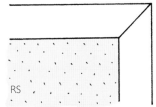

Detail of Avril Ellis' attractive Victorian-inspired quilt, which features a striking plaited border.

ACKNOWLEDGMENTS

My thanks go to the following people. To Cheryl Brown at David & Charles, who is kind enough to ask me to write books, which add to the Pension Fund.

To Lin Clements, who edits my words so well and makes everything smooth and easy.

To my friend Heather Jackson, who lets me bounce ideas off her and often comes up with much better ones of her own that she lets me use. To Verona at Sew and So's in Bungay, Suffolk for the supply of fabric for the classes in the Hall in Chelsworth and for the projects in this book. Her choices are a constant temptation and source of inspiration to us all. Tel: 01986 896147. www.sewsos.co.uk

To all the quilters in Chelsworth, who test out all my ideas and designs without ever demanding a fee – as yet . . .

To the team at Creative Grids, who make it possible for me to cut a straight piece of fabric. Tel: 0845 4507722. www.creativegrids.com

ABOUT THE AUTHOR

Lynne Edwards teaches and demonstrates a wide range of patchwork and quilting techniques, both hand and machine. She has written several textbooks that are considered to be definitive works. Her previous books for David & Charles are *The Sampler Quilt Book* (1996), *The New Sampler Quilt Book* (2000) and *Making Scrap Quilts to Use It Up* (2003).

In 1992 Lynne was awarded the Jewel Pearce Patterson Scholarship for International Quilt Teachers. This is in recognition of outstanding qualities as a teacher and included a trip to the Houston Quilt Market and Festival. The award led to invitations to teach as part of the Houston Faculty in 1993 and 1995 and at the Symposium of the Australasian Quilters' Guild in Brisbane in 1993. Since then international teaching trips have included venues in Europe, in Missouri, and the National Quilt Show in South Africa. In 2000, teaching commitments included Durban in South Africa and the National Canadian Festival, Canada 2000.

Her long association with the quilting movement both locally and nationally has involved Lynne in the organization of quilt shows, from a local village hall to the Quilters' Guild National Exhibitions. She has served on selection committees and is an experienced judge of National Quilt Shows. She was Senior Judge at the South African National Quilt Show in 1998, her first experience of judging overseas. In 2000, Lynne was given honorary lifetime membership of the Quilters' Guild of the British Isles and in 2002 was awarded the Amy Emms Memorial Trophy for services to quilting.

Index

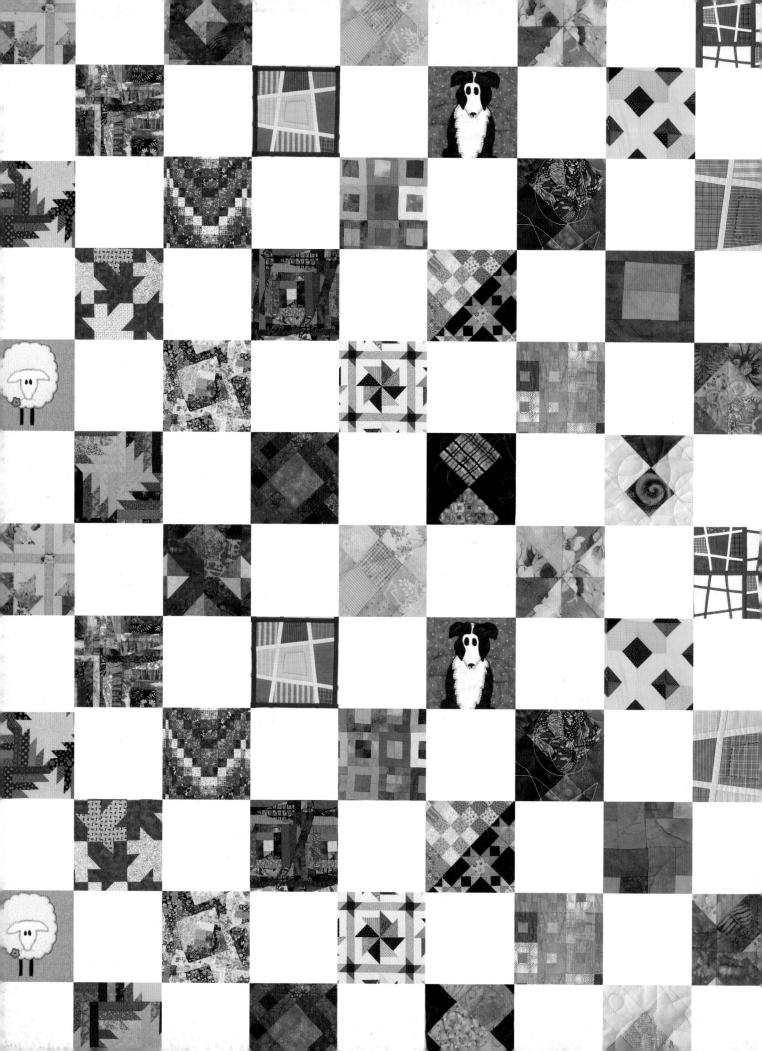

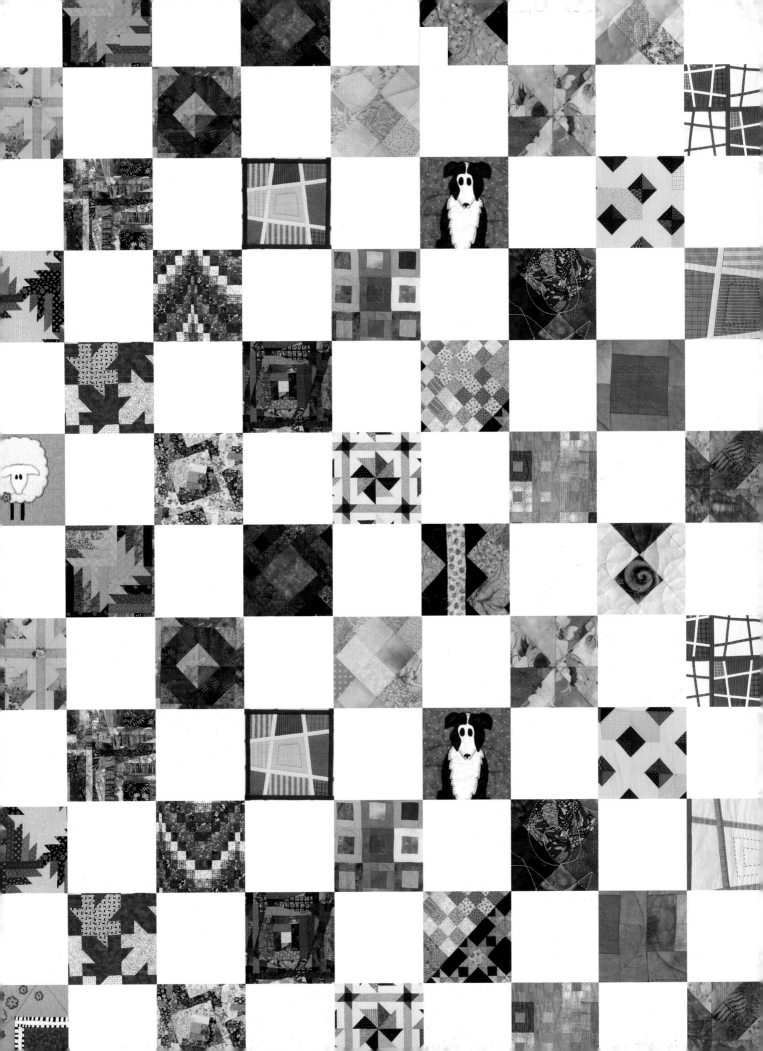